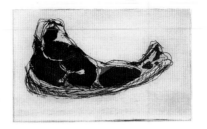

PRIME CUTS

Sonia Stevenson

PRIME CUTS

Sumptuous, succulent, sizable — the last word in steak

CONTEMPORARY BOOKS

A Quintet book

Published in the United States in 2000 by
Contemporary Books
A division of NTC/Contemporary Publishing
Group, Inc.
4255 West Touhy Avenue
Lincolnwood (Chicago), Illinois 60712-1975
U.S.A.

ISBN 0-8092-2441-0

Library of Congress Cataloguing-in-Publication
Data is available from the United States Library
of Congress.

This book was designed and produced by
Quintet Publishing Limited
6 Blundell Street
London N7 9BH

Creative Director: Richard Dewing

Art Director: Simon Daley

Designer: Paul Wright

Food stylist: Julz Beresford

Photographer: Paola Zucchi

Senior Editor: Sally Green

Editor: Anna Bennett

Typeset in Great Britain by
Central Southern Typesetters, Eastbourne
Manufactured in Hong Kong by
Regent Publishing Services Ltd
Printed in China by
Leefung-Asco Printers Ltd

Note
Because of the risk of salmonella poisoning, raw
or lightly cooked eggs should not be served to
the very young, the ill or elderly, or to pregnant
women.

The author would like to thank
Philip Warren for his help and advice.

Contents

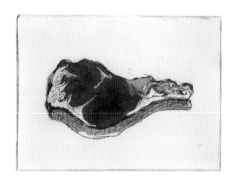

Introduction

It is blissfully simple to cook a delicious juicy steak in a matter of minutes and satisfy even the most demanding person. If you start with a good-quality cut of steak, all you need is a strong source of heat, some seasoning, and a little know-how from this book, and you will have the ingredients for a perfect result. Not only that, but you will be providing someone with a nutritious helping of minerals, fiber, and vitamins–among the most essential ingredients for good health.

While I ran my own restaurant, I always offered a steak dish, which changed as often as I changed the menu. But it was only when I threw away my carving knife and took up my pen that I realized how many different ways there are to cook this most adaptable piece of meat.

Some of my best recipes have come from having run out of some ingredient or other, and having to make a substitution and do a little experimenting. Cooking is a living, ever-developing art; no sooner have you cooked something than it's eaten and you start afresh with a clean slate, and a new idea or recipe. The great thing is to enjoy the challenge and you will be rewarded one hundred-fold by the appreciation you receive.

What makes a steak tender

To enjoy the experience of cooking steak, and to gain the confidence to experiment with different cuts, it is useful to have some background information about the quality of beef to enable you to make the most of selected luxury cuts.

Steaks are taken from the muscle tissue (or "meat" as it is called), the natural purpose of which is to move parts of the animal.

Lean beef is composed of approximately 18 percent protein, 3 percent fat, and 75 percent water. The protein part is both the fiber in the steak and the pigment as well, which means that the color of the meat as it cooks indicates the temperature it has reached and thus how well-done it is. Up to 140°F meat is still red but then it starts to cook and color. At 160°F it is pink and medium; but when the temperature reaches 175°F the steak is a brownish gray color and well done.

The fat content is very important. It needs to be mingled with the red meat, producing an effect called "marbling." This "oils" the meat during cooking and makes for a more tender steak. It also produces flavor.

Finally, the water content determines whether a steak will be dry or juicy. Freshly cut meat releases its juices as it cooks. When fierce heat from a broiler or a barbecue is applied to a steak, the steak fibers contract and squeeze out the juices. These caramelize on the surface, producing an intensely flavored crust. The more the meat is cooked, the drier the inside becomes and the more flavorful the outside; the juices, however, are not sealed in, which is why it is very difficult to produce a juicy well-done steak.

The quality of beef is improved by hanging at temperatures between 34°F and 38°F for between 10 days to 3 weeks, which tenderizes the meat and intensifies its flavor. During this time a certain amount of moisture is lost and because this contributes to the total carcass weight, the resulting loss of weight is an expensive exercise from a butcher's point of view and is reflected in the retail price.

As far as quality is concerned, the actual raising of the animal is crucial. British cattle are more often matured slowly on pasture and develop a firm texture and incomparable flavor. American cattle are usually enclosed in pens for their final 10 weeks or so. This inhibits movement and allows a high-grain diet to be administered, producing very tender and flavorful meat.

Regardless of the overall quality of the meat, steaks will vary both in tenderness and flavor according to their position on the carcass. The more work any muscle has to perform, the tougher it will be and cuts of meat intended for quick steak-cooking, therefore, come from the less active muscles in the animal.

Cuts of steak

Although nature has given all cattle the same structure, the size and proportions of the breed, the method of raising, and the tradition of butchering all result in differences in what cuts are retailed. In addition, a particular cut may have one name in one part of the country and a different name in another, and to complete the picture a name used in one place may denote a different cut in another.

Many supermarkets are circumventing the problem by labeling meat simply "for braising," "for broiling," "for frying" or "for grilling." While this makes life simpler, it denies the more adventurous cook the facility of choosing a particular cut for a particular purpose.

Although most recipes will work for a number of cuts of steak, a little understanding of the cuts of meat is very useful.

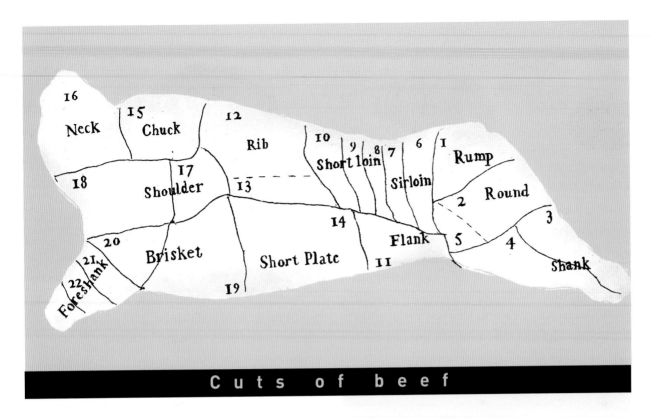

Cuts of beef

Chuck steak The cheapest steaks, taken from the shoulder, need to be "seam cut." The shoulder muscle is part of a group commonly called chuck steak and often for convenience is included in the meat used for braising. They are most tender when cooked rare and toughen progressively and swiftly the longer they cook so are not recommended for well-done steaks. The texture is loose but incredibly juicy and full of flavor–well worth buying if you can find a butcher who will produce the genuine article!

Hanger, hanging tender, or hanging tenderloin steak
This unusual steak is colloquially called the "slaughterman's perk" because it hangs down separately from the main carcass near the kidney. It is now always removed with the offal and therefore only available by order from wholesalers or butchers with their own abattoirs. The whole piece of meat weighs 1½ to 2 lb. When it is trimmed and the sinews dividing the meat are removed it falls into two pieces, each weighing about 10 oz, looking rather like two thick pork tenderloins. Very

1 Rolled rump, standing rump

2 Round steak, top round, bottom round

3 Heel of round

4 Hind shank

5 Tip steak or roast

6 Sirloin steak

6, 7, 8 & 9 Tenderloin or fillet

8 Porterhouse steak

9 T-bone steak

10 Club steak

11 Rolled flank and flank meat, flank steak and fillets

12 Standing rib roast, rib steak, rolled rib roast

13 Short rib

14 Rolled plate, plate "boiling"

15 Blade steak, blade pot roast, boneless chuck (pot roast), triangle pot roast

16 Rolled neck, boneless neck

17 English cut

18 Rolled shoulder, arm steak

19 Corned beef

19, 20 Brisket

21 Shank knuckle

22 Cross cut foreshank

Left to right: Fillet Steak, Rolled Rump, Tournedos, T-Bone Steak.

juicy and flavorful, it is tender when cooked rare. For pan-frying, grilling, or broiling.

Porterhouse steak There are only two of these steaks in one hindquarter of the carcass. The backbone is large and prominent with little of the T left, but the fillet here is enormous and if boned out and sliced would produce the Chateaubriand steak. The top part of the meat has an edging of fat and gristle, and is of inferior quality to the T-bone because it has a seam or curve of gristle cutting into the steak. Above this seam the meat has a rump-like quality, so there are three textures of steak in one cut. Porterhouse steak is best broiled or grilled.

Rib eye steak/Rib eye roast This cut is found toward the neck of the rib section, next to the chuck. The meat is of moderate tenderness and when well-trimmed makes an acceptable steak of looser texture. It is the cut that is well suited for frying.

Rib steak This type of steak must be seam-cut. The eye of the ribs and the piece of muscle attached to it have to be cut away from the rib bones in one piece. To do this the thick tendon ("back strap"), top strip of meat, and all outside fat are removed. The rib steak is then trimmed of a thin sheet of gristle (or connective tissue, as it is called) and sliced into steaks. On request it can be butchered with a rib bone attached, then trimmed as above and cooked and served as a double steak.

A slice taken from between the bones should be called an entrecôte (which means, literally, "between the ribs"), but this term is now more often used to denote any steak taken from the rib or loin. This is a tender steak with good flavor, suitable for broiling, grilling, or frying.

Round steak Used as steak meat in the United States where, because of the way the meat is raised, this cut is sufficiently tender. There are six major sections into which the round can be divided: the rump; the four main muscles (top round, sirloin tip, bottom round, and eye of round); and the heel. In Britain, supermarkets recommend that it should be pan-fried or roasted and many people use it in this way, since there are no seams or fat, but it makes a very tough steak. It can be needled to tenderize it.

Short loin steaks The short loin is the most tender of the major wholesale cuts of beef. It lies in the middle of the back between the sirloin and the rib, and the two main muscles in the cut are the tenderloin and the top loin. The tenderloin, when separated from the bone and the rest of the short loin, can be sold as tenderloin roasts (often labeled Chateaubriand) or alternatively cut into tournedos or filet mignon steaks.

The top loin muscle, with bone attached, is the "club steak," and when removed, this same muscle is sold as New York, strip steak, or Delmonico steak. With the bone still in place and parts of both the tenderloin and top loin muscles included, the short loin produces T-bone and Porterhouse steaks.

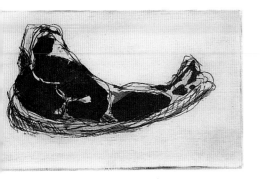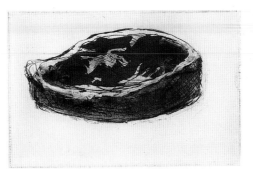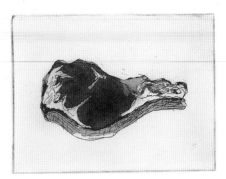

Left to right: Porterhouse Steak, Chateaubriand, Sirloin Steak.

Sirloin steak The sirloin lies between the very tender short loin and the tougher rump and round (see above). Sirloin is usually cut into steaks or roasts. Without the bone, the cuts are named for the three main muscles: top sirloin, a continuation of the tender top loin muscle of the short loin; tenderloin, part of the tenderest muscle (which continues from the short loin); and the bottom sirloin, part of the same, but less tender, sirloin tip muscle found in the round. In order of tenderness, the best known bone-in steaks are: pinbone, flat bone, round bone, and wedge bone.

Sirloin butt steak At the rump end of the sirloin, steaks are traditionally cut from this large triangular-shaped piece of meat by slicing across the grain in big swathes right down to the tip. However, there is now a move to seam-cut, slicing the muscles individually. Butchered in this way there are slices which have no top fat–perhaps an advantage for some people. The meat is slightly tough but of excellent flavor and is suitable for broiling, pan-frying, and grilling. It is sometimes braised, but is usually considered too expensive for this kind of treatment.

T-bone steaks These huge steaks incorporate both the sirloin and the tenderloin in one large slice with the bone attached. They are of better quality than the similar Porterhouse steaks, since they do not incorporate the seam of gristle found in the latter. However, the fillet steak or undercut here is of medium size. If boned and cut into slices, they would be called tournedos steaks, an interesting form of steak containing back fat, sirloin, and undercut all in one portion. Some restaurants cheat and serve a slice of sirloin and a slice of fillet, without any bone attached, and call it a T-bone. Both tender and textured at the same time, T-bone steaks are usually broiled but could be roasted if liked. It is an expensive cut of meat.

Tenderloin This meat is the most tender muscle in the animal. It is usually seam-cut from the carcass, but see T-bone and Porterhouse.

The narrow end nearest the ribs of the carcass is called the filet mignon. It is either sliced into thin pieces and cooked for seconds over high heat, ground and used for expensive hamburgers and steak tartare, or made into tiny steaks and butterflied open.

The next section of the muscle provides the tournedos steaks. It is the most sought-after part of the animal being even in thickness and very tender. This cut is often cooked whole in pastry.

The next section provides the two Chateaubriand steaks. These are traditionally cut very thick, 2 in at least, and are large.

Finally, the hip end of the muscle becomes a bit ragged. It needs trimming and these sections are used in the same way as described for the mignon end.

The whole tenderloin muscle can be lacking in flavor, but being such a tender cut this is used to advantage by restaurants who pride themselves on their sauces.

Cooking methods

Grilling The heat source for this method of cooking, typically at temperatures between 2000°F and 3000°F, is usually situated several inches below the meat and can be supplied by gas, electricity, or charcoal. The distance the steak is placed above the source controls the amount of heat concentrated on its surface and a certain amount of skill is needed to regulate this heat to produce the required searing effect without burning the meat. A drip tray to catch dripping fat is sometimes built into the appliance to prevent the hazard of burning hot oil spitting out and injuring people.

An overhead grill produces a similar effect as long as it can supply enough heat. A domestic broiler is not sufficient.

Barbecuing chars and flavors the meat during the cooking process. Brushing the meat with oil in advance or basting the meat during cooking adds to the flavor and improves the texture.

Pan-frying or Sautéeing As the meat is in direct contact with the skillet, the temperature of the heat source can be much lower than with grilling. A layer of fat lies between the skillet and the meat to prevent sticking and its temperature is typically in the region of 450°F for oil or 325°F for butter. Excess fat or oil must be poured off during cooking or the meat will deep-fry.

This method produces a delicious crust on the meat and some residual juices which make a base for sauces and gravies.

Broiling or roasting This heat source is supplied by convection from the walls of the appliance. It is a drying heat and takes longest to penetrate the thickness of the meat and is used for larger pieces of steak such as whole tenderloin or sirloin which require slower cooking. Meat is often seared in a pan to produce a full-flavored crust on the exterior of the joint, before being placed in the oven. The temperature is regulated from 450°F to start and turned down to 300°F to complete the process.

Microwaving The effect of the waves is to penetrate the meat to about ¾ inch and cook by friction. Further deeper penetration of heat is effected by conduction, and meat will continue to cook after it is removed from the heat source.

Although a certain amount of juices will be extruded from the meat, the result is similar to the meat having been poached. This method is most useful when a well-done steak is required, because the cooking is very quickly performed and produces a steak running with juices. To prevent the boiled appearance, the meat should first be seared over high heat to produce a crust and then transferred to the microwave oven.

Deep-frying A coating of some kind must cover the meat for this method of cooking, because lowering it into hot fat will not brown it in a satisfactory manner. Meat cooked inside a coating, however, will retain more moisture and be uniquely succulent.

Braising This method of cooking is reserved for tougher cuts of steak that would benefit from longer cooking. Obviously, the meat will be well-done. The secret is never to allow the cooking temperature to rise above 185°F. Above this heat the fibers in the steak clench tight and the only way to release them is to stew them until they disintegrate. Bacteria are killed at about 158°F, so no health hazard is involved. The meat may be seared first.

NOTE **Unless otherwise stated, all recipes serve four.**

Cooking Times

All cooking appliances vary, so the following are guidelines only, and are mainly linked to thickness, not weight. Always pre-heat the appliance, and remember that off the heat the meat continues to cook for about another minute or so, especially the thicker cuts. This has been allowed for.

Cut	Size	Rare	Medium	Well-done
Short loin/entrecôte with no bone	1 inch thick	3½ minutes	5 minutes	7 minutes
	1½ inch thick	4½ minutes	6 minutes	8 minutes
Rib steak/entrecôte with bone in	1½ inch thick	6 minutes	8 minutes	12 minutes
T-bone	10 oz	8 minutes	12 minutes	18 minutes
T-bone from larger animal	20 oz	10 minutes	14 minutes	20 minutes
Filet mignon	1 inch thick	2½ minutes	4 minutes	8 minutes
Tournedos	1½ inch thick	5 minutes	8 minutes	12 minutes
	2 inch thick	8 minutes	12 minutes	20 minutes
Tenderloin in oven	whole	24 minutes	35 minutes	45 minutes

Marinades

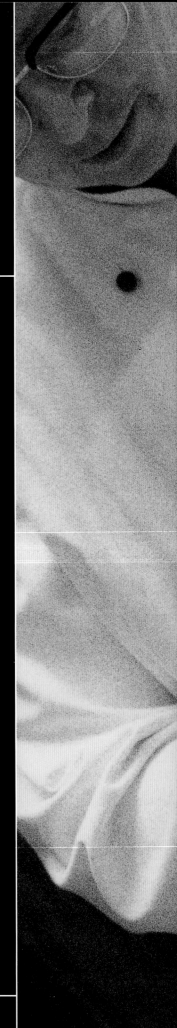

IT IS WONDERFUL HOW YOU CAN ALTER THE TEXTURE

AND FLAVOR OF THE SIMPLEST PIECE OF STEAK JUST BY

LAYING IT IN A FEW SPICES OR SOME WINE OR JUICES

FOR A COUPLE OF HOURS. LONGER MARINATING WILL

HELP TO TENDERIZE A TOUGH PIECE AND PRESERVE IT,

TOO. THE FLAVOR PENETRATES SLOWLY SO IT'S BEST TO

START IN PLENTY OF TIME. CHOOSE A COOKED RED

WINE MARINADE FOR A SOPHISTICATED FLAVOR AND AN

UNCOOKED ONE FOR GAMEY FLAVORS. ONE OF THE BEST

WAYS TO MARINATE IS TO PUT THE MIXED INGREDIENTS

IN A PLASTIC BAG, ADD THE MEAT, AND SEAL THE BAG.

SHAKE IT AROUND TO MAKE SURE THAT EVERY BIT OF

MEAT IS COVERED AND STORE IN THE REFRIGERATOR.

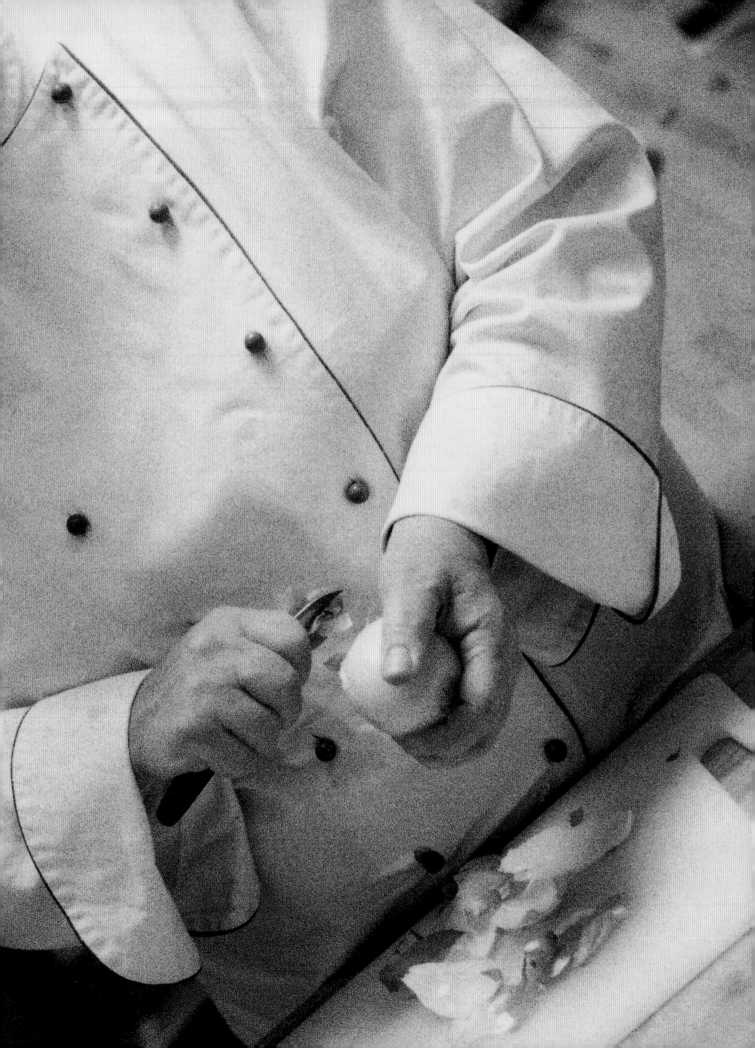

Cooked marinade

When wine is cooked, it loses its alcohol, leaving a mature reduction behind, which gives a depth of flavor to the meat.

1¾ cups red or white wine

¼ cup wine vinegar

1 onion, sliced

1 carrot, diced

1 celery stick, sliced

12 black peppercorns, crushed

6 juniper berries, crushed

3 Tbsp vegetable oil

¼ cup olive oil

Simmer all the ingredients together except for the olive oil for 20 minutes. Cool. Strain while still just warm then whisk in the olive oil. This marinade tenderizes the meat.

Uncooked marinade

This marinade imparts a flavor similar to game. Of course, it is really only because tough game is rendered tender by aging in wine that this association occurs.

1 onion, chopped

½ cup red or white wine

1 Tbsp wine vinegar

1 tsp crushed black peppercorns

½ tsp salt

3 Tbsp olive oil

Mix all the ingredients together for a marinade that will add flavor to the meat.

Mustard marinade

If you want a coating with a gentle "kick" this is the marinade to use. It penetrates the meat and livens up a plain steak.

2 tsp freshly ground mixed peppercorns

¼ cup grapeseed oil

2 garlic cloves, minced

2 tsp ground ginger

¼ cup wholegrain mustard

1 Tbsp brown sugar

Mix all the ingredients together for a flavorful marinade.

▶ Top left: Cooked marinade
Top right: Uncooked marinade
Bottom: Mustard marinade

Tomato marinade

Just the job for the outdoor barbecue. A traditional recipe with a universal appeal.

1 garlic clove, minced

¼ cup tomato catsup

¼ cup soy sauce

¼ cup vegetable oil

1 Tbsp sugar

1 Tbsp red wine vinegar

½ tsp Worcestershire sauce

1 tsp ground cumin

½ tsp chili powder

½ tsp English mustard powder

Salt and pepper

Mix all the ingredients together and coat the steaks with the mixture before grilling or broiling.

◄ Top left: Three-juice marinade
Top right: Quick marinade
Bottom: Tomato marinade

3-juice marinade

Served chilled, unused, extra amounts of this marinade make a delicious drink.

½ cup orange juice

½ cup tomato juice

½ cup pineapple juice

¼ cup vegetable oil

1-in piece fresh ginger root, peeled and crushed

½ tsp allspice

1 tsp chili flakes

Mix all the ingredients together and marinate the meat in it for 8 hours or overnight.

Quick marinade

Don't leave the meat in this mixture for more than 30 minutes—it's too strong.

¼ cup dark soy sauce

¼ cup red wine

¼ cup vegetable oil

2 garlic cloves, minced

1 tsp Tabasco or chili sauce

Mix all the ingredients together and marinate the meat in it for no more than a half hour. Pat dry.

Curry marinade

After the initial searing of the meat, turn the heat down and cook the steaks gently in this marinade, or the delicate spicy flavor will be lost.

Pinch of cinnamon

½ tsp curry powder

Pinch of ground cumin

½ tsp paprika

1 tsp ground coriander

20 cardamom seeds

2 garlic cloves, minced

½ cup plain yogurt

Mix all the ingredients together until well-combined.

Hot rubs

Both these rubs have a strong spicy flavor, the milder being the wasabi. They give the steak a crisp exterior. Use 1 teaspoon of the mixture to every 8 oz of meat to begin with; increase the quantity when you have become accustomed to the spice.

WASABI PASTE RUB

2 tsp allspice

2 tsp ground cumin

2 tsp paprika

2 tsp dried basil leaves

1 Tbsp wasabi paste

½ tsp chili powder (or more, to taste)

1 tsp garlic salt

BLACK PEPPER RUB

2 Tbsp ground black pepper

2 tsp onion salt

2 tsp garlic salt

2 tsp paprika

1 tsp chili powder

1 tsp mustard powder

Broths & Bases

ALTHOUGH TIME-CONSUMING TO PREPARE, A GOOD

HOMEMADE BROTH OR SIMILAR BASE IS AN ESSENTIAL

FOUNDATION THAT WILL MAKE ALL THE DIFFERENCE TO

THE TEXTURE AND FLAVOR OF THE FINISHED DISH.

SOUPS WILL TASTE MORE WHOLESOME AND SAUCES WILL

HAVE A DEPTH OF FLAVOR THAT NO BOUGHT BROTH

CAN PROVIDE. A PLAIN STEAK CAN THUS BE DRESSED

FOR A LAVISH OCCASION. IF YOU CAN, INVEST IN A

STOCKPOT OR A SLOW COOKER FOR THE PURPOSE.

IT IS USEFUL TO KEEP A FEW BROTHS AND BASES IN

THE FREEZER READY TO USE WHENEVER REQUIRED.

Vegetable broth

The full flavor and lightness of a vegetable broth is a quality that no meat base can equal. Do not be tempted to add salt to this base; it can be added to the finished dish later on.

2 medium onions, sliced

2 leeks, trimmed of excess green

1 fennel bulb, sliced

3 strips orange peel, sliced

1 garlic clove, sliced

1 star anise

1 bay leaf

1 Tbsp peanut oil

1 Combine all the ingredients in a pan and sweat them together for 2 or 3 minutes. Add 4 cups cold water and bring to a boil. Simmer for 20 minutes.

2 Pour through a strainer, pressing out as much broth as possible.

Beef broth

There is no substitute for a homemade base, made from fresh ingredients. When you buy steak, ask for some bones as well and you may be lucky enough to get them free. If not, buy rib bones from boned and rolled joints and a couple of pounds of shin. Then, later on, you can lift out the shin when it is tender and grind, mince, or chop it finely and season it for stuffing tomatoes or making the Special ground beef and lentil chops (page 114).

10 lb beef bones

½ cup vegetable oil

2 lb foreshank, sliced

1 lb carrots, sliced

3 lb onions, sliced

2 celery sticks, chopped

3 leeks, chopped

2 lb fresh or canned tomatoes, chopped

1 bay leaf

2 thyme sprigs

6 parsley stalks

1 tsp dried thyme

1 Place the bones in a roasting pan and place in a hot oven, at about 375°F, until the fat and juices run and the meat browns.

2 Transfer the bones to a large pan or stock pot. Add the vegetables to the fat in the roasting pan, adding the oil if necessary, and fry them off to give them a good color, spooning them as they brown into the pan.

3 Pour off all fat and oil and rinse the roasting pan with a little water, scraping any brown bits clinging to the base. Add to the pan.

4 Put the shin in the pan. Cover with cold water, and bring to a boil. Skim off any scum as it rises. Reduce the heat and simmer for about 4 hours. Remove the shin now if you wish to use it for another dish otherwise continue to simmer the broth for a further 2 hours.

5 Remove the bones, strain the broth and chill overnight. Lift off any fat and reduce to a desired depth of flavor. Greatly reduced, it can be used as a beef glaze.

Special brown broth

When a good broth without a strong beef flavor is required, I use the ingredients in Beef broth (page 21) but include a balanced variety of bones, such as chicken and lamb as well. The true secret of good broth, apart from the quality of the ingredients, is that it must never vigorously boil, or the fat will emulsify and make the broth cloudy instead of clear. Meat cooks and gives off flavor best at 200°F. Vegetables, on the other hand, need to have been browned and par-cooked first.

1 Cut the foreshank into 1½-inch squares. Heat the oil in a skillet and brown the carrots, onions, celery, and leeks until they develop a good dark color.

2 Add the shank pieces and brown them as well, sprinkling on the thyme. Place the bones in the bottom of a stockpot or large pan.

3 Add the contents of the skillet and rinse the skillet with some water, scraping up all the brown residue. Add it to the stockpot with the tomatoes and herbs.

4 Cover with cold water, bring to a boil, skimming off and discarding the scum as it rises. Simmer gently for at least 4 hours. Strain and chill overnight. Lift off any fat, and reduce to a concentrated flavor. Freeze until required.

Parmesan meatballs with pasta and broth

The cheese flavor really comes through when you bite into these little morsels.

3 oz beef trimmings without fat or gristle

1 small egg, whisked

3 Tbsp grated Parmesan cheese

7 Tbsp fresh bread crumbs

2 tsp chopped fresh parsley

½ tsp salt

1 oz dried farfalline cooked in salted water

4 cups vegetable broth

1 garlic clove, minced

1 Tbsp olive oil

1 In a blender purée the meat and incorporate the egg, cheese, bread crumbs, parsley, and salt. Divide and roll the mixture into 20 small balls. Chill.

2 Heat the oil in a large pan, add the garlic and brown it. Add the broth, bring to a boil, and season. Drop in the balls and simmer for five minutes until cooked, then add the cooked pasta. Reheat, check the seasoning, and serve.

Fresh tomato purée

This is an indispensable recipe. It's the base of all tomato sauces and, being homemade, has a fresh flavor that no canned substitute can approach.

2 Tbsp vegetable or peanut oil

1 medium onion, chopped

1½ lb tomatoes, chopped

2 garlic cloves, minced

1 tsp dried thyme

1 bay leaf

6 parsley stalks

1 tsp sugar

Salt and pepper

1 Put the oil and onion in a nonstick pan, add ⅔ cup water and simmer until the water has evaporated and the onion begins to fry.

2 Add the tomatoes, garlic, thyme, bay leaf, parsley, and sugar and simmer for 40 minutes to mature and reduce, stirring from time to time to prevent the tomatoes from sticking to the base and burning. When the mixture is nearly dry, discard the bay leaf and blend to a purée in a blender. Check the seasoning and rub through a sifter to remove any seeds and tough skins.

French onion soup

A good base makes all the difference to this soup, which can become rather sweet without an adequate meat base.

8 oz onions, sliced

½ stick butter

4 cups beef broth

Salt and pepper

4 slices French bread

¼ cup grated Parmesan cheese

¼ cup grated Swiss cheese

1 Simmer the onions in the butter until soft and brown. Pour on the broth and season liberally. Simmer for 30 minutes then pour into deep individual ovenproof soup bowls.

2 Toast the bread and mix the two cheeses together. Pile the cheeses onto the toasted bread, lay them on top of the soups, and place under the broiler for 10 minutes until the cheese has melted.

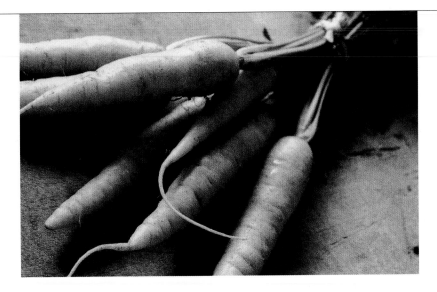

Vegetable soup with beef

Make sure the soup is very hot before the beef
goes in, or it won't cook.

1 Put the vegetables in a very deep pan and tuck the meat into the
middle of them. Cover generously with cold water, bring to a boil, season,
and simmer for 10 minutes. Reduce the heat, remove any scum which
rises to the top, and partially cover. Leave to cook for 2 hours.

2 Remove the meat carefully, so as not to break it up, and allow it to rest
for 5 minutes. Meanwhile, drain the vegetables, discarding the bay leaves.
Serve thick slices of beef with the vegetables and a little broth. Reserve
the strained broth for a beef soup.

2½ lb rolled chuck, preferably
in a net

1 large baking potato, peeled and
quartered

2 Spanish onions, quartered

4 carrots, sliced thick

3 celery stalks, sliced thick

1 small bunch parsley, chopped

2 large beef tomatoes, chopped

1 parsnip, peeled and sliced

6 large scallions, chopped

3 white turnips, peeled and sliced

1 large thyme sprig

2 bay leaves

¼ tsp chile flakes

20 black peppercorns, ground

1 tsp salt

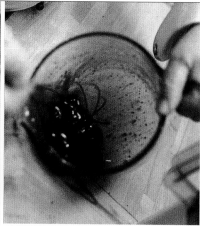

Beef soup

Sometimes soup on its own is not filling enough and the steak provides the extra protein needed on a cold day. This is the perfect dish in which to use up any trimmings from the Roast beef tenderloin on page 107. It is vital that the soup bowls are very hot so that the meat cooks a little when the soup is poured on top.

1 recipe Cooked marinade (page 14)

8 oz fillet steak, sliced

3¾ cups vegetable and beef broth, strained

Parsley leaves, to garnish

1 Season the meat and marinate for 2 hours. Drain, wipe dry, and place in hot soup bowls. Reduce the marinade to 2 tablespoons, add to the broth, and bring to a boil.

2 Check the seasoning, pour over the beef, and serve with a spoonful of Horseradish Sauce (see page 36) floating on top and the parsley leaves to garnish.

ALTERNATIVE: Omit the marinade, but season the broth carefully.

Steak and kidney soup

This makes a satisfying light lunch dish, especially with a bit of Stilton cheese crumbled over it as garnish.

1 Fry the onion until brown in the drippings or butter. Roll the kidney pieces in the flour and fry with the onions until browned. Pour on the broth, bring to a boil, stirring from time to time, and simmer for ¾ hour.

2 Lift out a few pieces of the kidney for garnish and purée the rest in a blender. Return the soup to the pan to reheat. As it comes to a boil slip in the filet mignon slices, garnish with the kidney pieces, season well with salt and pepper, and serve.

1 onion, chopped

1 Tbsp beef drippings or butter

½ lb beef kidney, cubed

2 Tbsp flour

4 cups beef broth

12 very thin slices filet mignon

Salt

Pepper

Sauces & Butters

SAUCES AND BUTTERS ADD THE FINISHING TOUCH TO

BRING OUT THE FLAVOR OF A GOOD STEAK AND

TANTALIZE THE TASTEBUDS. MOST OF THESE, MADE IN

ADVANCE OR WHIPPED UP AT THE LAST MOMENT, ARE

VERY LITTLE TROUBLE TO MAKE, AND MAKE GOOD

ACCOMPANIMENTS TO MOST STEAKS. WHERE A

PARTICULAR STEAK SUITS THE SAUCE HOWEVER, THE

STEAK IS INCLUDED IN THE RECIPE. ALSO,

THROUGHOUT THE BOOK SAUCES ARE SUGGESTED AS

ACCOMPANIMENTS TO VARIOUS DISHES. BUT OF COURSE,

THE CHOICE IS YOURS. WHERE SAUCES ARE INTEGRAL

TO A RECIPE, SUCH AS STEAK GRAND VENEUR AND SAUCE

GRAND VENEUR, OR CHARGRILLED FILLET STEAK WITH

SALSA VERDE, YOU WILL FIND THE RECIPE FOR THE

SAUCE WITH THAT PARTICULAR DISH.

Sauce béarnaise

This recipe makes a light béarnaise with an intense tarragon flavor. Pass it through a strainer when it is made to remove the cooked leaves and replace these with some fresh ones chopped fine, giving the sauce bright green flecks.

2 Tbsp chopped fresh tarragon

1 tsp dried tarragon

½ cup white wine tarragon-flavored vinegar

¼ stick butter

2 egg yolks (see page 4)

1 tsp water

1½ sticks unsalted butter

1 Chop the tarragon leaves and boil down with the dried tarragon in the vinegar with the ¼ stick butter until most of the kick has gone. Season and keep warm.

2 Melt the unsalted butter until it froths. Meanwhile, whisk the yolks and water together in a blender until pale. With a ladle, pour the butter through the hole in the lid of the blender a little at a time, pausing between each spoonful to allow the mixture to emulsify. Season to taste.

3 Whisk this sauce into the tarragon reduction. Serve warm.

Horseradish sauce

This must be made in large quantities or there won't be enough to go round. Because this version is so delicate, it can be eaten by the spoonful. Make it at least 30 minutes in advance to give it time to mature. Sadly, it doesn't keep for more than a day without losing its freshness.

2 Tbsp horseradish root

1 Tbsp malt vinegar

1 cup heavy cream

Pinch of salt

1 Scrape the fresh horseradish root clean and grate it fine.

2 Blend in first the malt vinegar and then the cream with a pinch of salt. Whisk until it begins to thicken.

3 Turn it into a bowl and allow to mature for at least 30 minutes, but for the best flavor not more than 6 hours. Keep cool but do not chill or the texture will harden.

▶ Follow the photographs overleaf for a full demonstration.

▶ Horseradish sauce

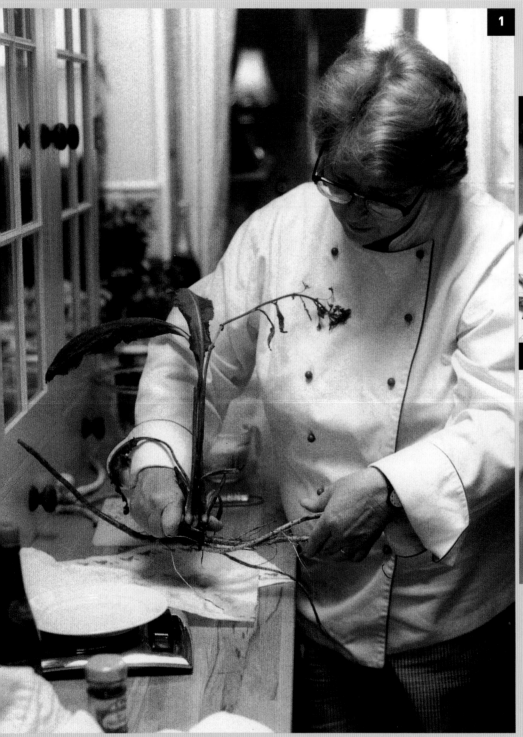

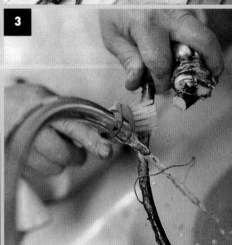

1, 2 & 3 Scrape the fresh horseradish root clean.
4 Grate it fine.
5 Blend in first the malt vinegar and then the
cream with a pinch of salt.
6 Whisk until the mixture begins to thicken.

S A U C E S & B U T T E R S 39

Top loin steak with aigroissade

This is a steak accompaniment for garlic lovers. The base is a stiff mayonnaise, heavily flavored with fresh garlic, and used to bind the canned garbanzos.

4 top loin steaks (weighing 8 oz each)

SAUCE:

2 egg yolks (see page 4)

4 garlic cloves, minced

1 tsp Dijon mustard

¼ tsp salt

1 cup olive oil

1 cup peanut oil

14-oz can garbanzos

1 Season and cook the steaks to your liking in a ridged griddle pan.

2 To make the aigroissade: make a thick mayonnaise by beating together the egg yolks, garlic, mustard, and salt. Pour in the oils, in a slow, steady trickle (it doesn't matter which one you add first) until the mixture emulsifies. Add the oil very slowly to begin with or the mayonnaise will separate.

3 Drain the garbanzos, fold into the mayonnaise, and serve a large spoonful with each steak, along with the vegetables of your choice.

Steak with sauce choron

The pungent, rich sauce makes a perfect accompaniment to the meat—or should it be the other way around? The tomatoes accentuate the flavor of the sauce.

SAUCE:

¾ cup tarragon vinegar

1 Tbsp chopped fresh tarragon

2 tsp chopped onion

1 Tbsp beef broth (page 22)

2 egg yolks (see page 4)

1 tsp tomato paste

4 sticks unsalted butter

½ tsp salt

4 sirloin butt steaks (weighing 10 oz each)

1 Bring the vinegar, tarragon, and onion to a boil and reduce the mixture until it begins to fry. Add the beef glaze and 3 tablespoon hot water. Transfer the mixture to a blender and add the egg yolks and tomato paste. Blend for one minute.

2 Meanwhile, melt the butter until it boils, then allow it to stand while the milk solids fall to the base. Switch on the blender and, using only the oily part of the butter, pour it over the yolk mixture through the lid 1 tablespoonful at a time until it is all incorporated, but leaving the milky part behind to be discarded. Add the salt.

3 Chargrill the steaks and serve them with Stuffed Tomatoes (page 58). Hand round the sauce separately.

Imam bayildi kabob or steak sauce

There are many versions of this sauce. If you like, add some cinnamon and canned tomatoes to the sauce before liquidizing.

4 eggplants

1 Tbsp olive oil

1½ sticks unsalted butter

2 garlic cloves, minced

Salt and pepper

1 tsp lemon juice or to taste

1 Preheat the oven to 400°F. Coat the eggplants with the oil and bake them until done, about 40 minutes. Slit them open and scrape out the flesh, discarding the skin.

2 Turn them into a blender while still warm, and mix in the butter, garlic, and seasoning. Add the lemon a little at a time to get the right balance.

Green peppercorn sauce

This is a more pungent peppercorn sauce than the one on page 72 for Steak au poivre with cream sauce. It can be made in advance and reheated in the pan that the steaks are cooked in, just before serving.

1 tsp butter

1 Tbsp peppercorn juice from can

1½ Tbsp cognac

2 Tbsp white wine

2 Tbsp canned green peppercorns, drained

1½ cups beef broth (page 22)

4 Tbsp crème fraîche or sour cream

Salt

1 In the skillet in which the steaks have been cooked, add the butter, pepper juice, cognac, and wine and simmer until there is only 1 tablespoon left.

2 Add the well-drained peppercorns, then the broth, and reduce to three-quarters of a cup.

3 Add the crème fraîche and salt to taste, bring to a boil and serve with the steaks.

VARIATION: See Green peppercorn steaks, page 87.

Onion gravy

Many dishes need moistening, and making a good onion sauce yourself extends the quality and quantity of the sauce. A thousand times better than the commercial packet variety!

3 medium onions, sliced thin

1 Tbsp beef drippings

2 tsp cornstarch mixed with 1 Tbsp water

1 cup good beef broth or gravy

Salt and pepper

1 Cook the onions slowly in the drippings until soft, allowing them to color but adding a little water if they become too dark. This should take about 30 minutes.

2 Add the cornstarch mixture and broth or gravy, bring to a boil, and simmer for five minutes. Season. There should now be 1¼ cups of the onion sauce.

Barbecue sauce dip

I'm very fond of this dip, which is like a reliable old friend.

3 Tbsp vegetable oil

3 Tbsp soy sauce

4 Tbsp tomato catsup

1 Tbsp sugar

1 Tbsp red wine vinegar

1 tsp ground cumin

1 tsp chili powder or dried chile flakes

1 tsp dry mustard powder

Dash of Worcestershire sauce

1 Mix all the ingredients well in a pan.

2 Bring to a boil and simmer for one minute. Chill and serve as required.

Red bell pepper sauce

Make this sauce as mild or hot as you like by adjusting the amount of chile you use, it tastes as good either way.

2 red bell peppers

1 red chile, sliced

2 cloves garlic

1 cup canned plum tomatoes

1 cup olive oil

2 Tbsp red wine vinegar

½ tsp salt

1 Tbsp ground hazelnuts

1 Tbsp ground almonds

1 Broil or otherwise char the bell peppers and peel them, discarding their seeds. In a nonstick pan mix together the chile, garlic, tomatoes, and peppers, and dry the mixture out, allowing it to brown a little.

2 Empty the mixture into a blender, add the olive oil, vinegar, and salt and purée until smooth. Mix in the ground nuts to thicken the sauce. Season.

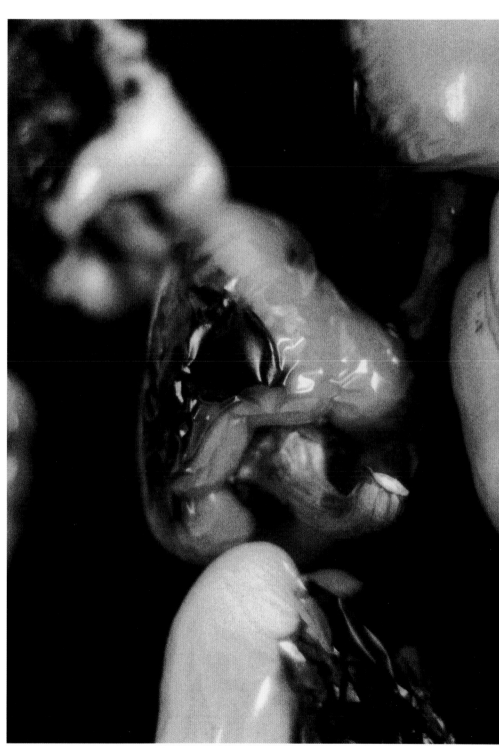

Hazelnut sauce

This sauce goes well
with Italian dishes,
especially meat balls.

2 cups roasted hazelnuts

¾ cup pine nuts

2 cloves garlic, minced

1 cup olive oil

⅓ cup grated Parmesan cheese

Salt to taste

1 Blend the hazelnuts, pine nuts,
garlic, and olive oil together.

2 Once the mixture is well
blended, mix in the grated
Parmesan and salt, and season
to taste.

Espagnole sauce (basic brown sauce)

The quality of a wine sauce is wholly dependent on the meat base it is made from. Many famous chefs insist that broth be made from veal bones exclusively but I find that a mixture of meat bones and some chicken carcasses, which gives the required gelatinous texture, is very satisfactory. Brown the vegetables slowly and well to give a good color.

3 Tbsp vegetable oil

1 lb onions, sliced fine

8 oz carrots, sliced fine

2 celery stalks, sliced fine

1 small leek, sliced fine

1½ Tbsp flour

½ stick butter

1 lb ripe or canned tomatoes, chopped

Mushroom peelings

½ tsp dried thyme

1 bay leaf

8 cups hot brown broth

1 Brown the onions, carrots, celery, and leek in the oil in a large, heavy pan. Brown the flour separately in a little of the butter to a golden color and add it to the onion mixture. Stir in the tomatoes, mushroom peelings, and herbs.

2 Add the hot broth, bring to a boil, and leave to simmer for three or four hours. Remove any scum occasionally and top up with more broth or water if the pan seems to be becoming a little dry.

3 Strain the liquid, or Espagnole sauce as it now is, and rinse the vegetables with a little water for a "second pressing." Add this to the sauce and reduce if necessary. Do not add salt. Add more broth at this point if the Espagnole needs a meatier flavor. Try to achieve a delicious basic flavor without too much of any one flavor predominating.

4 For a really rich sauce base you may add another pint of broth thickened with 2 tablespoons cornstarch to 2½ cups broth. Reduce to a more concentrated form, especially if you are going to store it in the freezer. Just add water to reconstitute it.

5 The Espagnole sauce is now ready for use as a base for gravies or red wine sauces. Chill, cube, and deep-freeze if you wish to store it.

Tarragon butter

A cold alternative to Sauce béarnaise that can be made in advance and tastes wonderful as it melts onto a hot steak.

1 stick unsalted butter

1 Tbsp lemon juice

2 Tbsp chopped fresh tarragon

1 tsp tarragon mustard

Salt and pepper

1 Cream the butter and add the other ingredients. Mix them together well.

2 Turn the butter onto plastic wrap and shape into a thin log. Chill. Slice as required.

Roquefort butter

No other cheese gives this depth of flavor to a butter, and melted on a hot steak it's irresistible.

Equal quantities unsalted butter and Roquefort cheese

1 Blend the two ingredients together thoroughly. Roll into a cylinder shape in plastic wrap and chill.

2 Add rounds of this flavored butter to cooked steak, and allow them to melt over the cooked steaks.

Maître d'hôtel butter

A famous butter that looks as good as it tastes good. It goes with almost everything from vegetables to steak or fish.

1 stick unsalted butter

1 Tbsp lemon juice

3 Tbsp chopped fresh parsley

Salt and pepper

1 Cream the butter in a food processor and add the other ingredients. Roll in foil into a sausage shape and chill. Alternatively, cream the butter, then blanch the parsley leaves in boiling water for 5 seconds, drain, and pat dry. While still warm, add them to the butter with seasoning to taste. Roll in foil and chill as above.

2 Add rounds of this flavored butter to cooked steak, and allow them to melt over the meat.

Garlic butter

Raw garlic can be overpoweringly pungent. Cook it, and it becomes a gentle giant, full of flavor without the sting.

1 garlic bulb

1 stick butter

1 cup water

1 Tbsp parsley, chopped fine (optional)

½ tsp salt

¼ tsp coarse ground pepper

1 Separate the cloves of garlic, mince in their skins with a cleaver, and discard the skins. In a small pan melt a piece of the butter and add the water and garlic. Simmer very gently for about an hour, adding a little more water if the pan becomes too dry but finally allowing the liquid to become syrupy. Allow to cool.

2 Cream the remaining butter in a food processor and blend in the garlic and parsley, if using. Season and wrap up in a cylinder shape in plastic wrap. Chill and slice as required.

Marchand de vin butter

The color of this butter is beautiful; the flavor even better, like having a glass of good red wine with your dish.

¼ stick butter

1 Tbsp fine chopped red onion

½ cup red wine

Pepper

1 stick unsalted butter

2 tsp lemon juice

2 tsp chopped parsley (optional)

¼ tsp salt

1 tsp Worcestershire sauce

1 Soften the onion in the ¼ stick butter, pour in the wine, and reduce it until the liquid has an oily appearance and most of the wine has been absorbed into the onion. Season generously with pepper and set the mixture aside to cool.

2 Meanwhile, cream the unsalted butter in a food processor, add the onion mixture, lemon juice, parsley, if using, salt, and Worcestershire sauce, and blend in. Roll into a cylinder shape in plastic wrap and chill. Melt slices of the flavored butter as required over cooked steak.

▶ Garlic butter

Garnishes

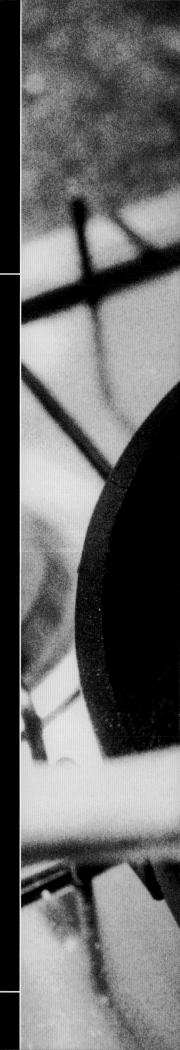

TRY TO CHOOSE A GARNISH THAT COMPLEMENTS THE

TYPE OF DISH YOU ARE PRESENTING—POLENTA FOR

ITALY; FRIED CELERY FOR ASIA; ONIONS FOR ENGLAND

AND SO ON. COLOR IS ALSO AN IMPORTANT FACTOR, SO

THERE ARE SOME EYE-CATCHING GARNISHES IN THIS

SECTION AS WELL.

Mixed vegetable salad

Made in advance and kept in the marinade, this salad matures and tastes all the better.

MARINADE:

1¼ cup olive oil

1 rosemary sprig

1 thyme sprig

3 garlic cloves, chopped

2 shallots, chopped fine

¼ cup sherry vinegar

1 red bell pepper, 1 green bell
pepper, and 1 yellow bell pepper,
cut into 6

3 zucchini, cut in thick rounds

2 eggplants, sliced in rounds

½ cup olive oil, to fry

1 small celery root, cut into
julienne strips

8 oz mushrooms, quartered

¼ cup balsamic vinegar

1 Mix all the marinade ingredients together in a saucepan and heat through. Set aside.

2 Wipe the bell peppers, heat a seared griddle pan, and sear the bell peppers slightly. Set aside. Then brown the zucchini and eggplant rounds in the same way. Set the vegetables aside.

3 In a large pan, heat the frying oil and add the celery root and mushrooms. Cook for 3 minutes, then add the bell peppers, zucchini, and eggplant, and cook briefly to soften them a little.

4 Pour over the marinade mixture. Stir in the balsamic vinegar. Allow to cool. Remove the rosemary and thyme sprigs and drain before serving. Store in the refrigerator.

Lemon mushrooms

Mushrooms can taste very insipid when sautéed as a garnish, but if you acidulate them with lemon juice it transforms them. Remember to season them well. A teaspoon of chopped fresh parsley brightens up the presentation.

8 oz closed cap mushrooms, sliced in half

¼ stick butter

½ tsp lemon juice

Salt and pepper

Lemon slices to serve

1 Sweat the mushroom halves in the butter for 1 minute.

2 Add 2 tablespoons water to the lemon juice and pour this over the mushrooms adding some salt and pepper.

3 Turn up the heat and cook until dry. Serve as a garnish with the lemon slices.

Onions and sauce soubise

Cooked onion develops a natural sweetness that softens other aggressive flavors, making it a gentle accompaniment to any steak dish.

1 If you are using the baby onions, simmer them unpeeled for five minutes in water, then cut away the base and squeeze the whole onion out of the sprouting end, or carefully peel each one. Set aside and discard water.

2 Sweat the sliced onions in half the butter until soft, then simmer them in the broth, with the whole baby onions. Remove the baby onions when they are done and purée the rest in a blender.

3 When the mixture is smooth, add the cream and the remaining butter. Check the seasoning.

4 Return the sauce to the pan to boil off excess liquid if the sauce is too thin then add the baby onions.

12 baby onions (optional)

2 medium onions, sliced

1 stick unsalted butter

1 cup seasoned vegetable broth

½ cup heavy cream

Salt and pepper

Stuffed tomatoes

These tomatoes add another dimension to a pan-fried steak by creating a contrasting texture and flavor.

1 boneless chicken breast, cooked

½ cup heavy cream

1 tsp cornstarch mixed with a little water

¼ tsp ground nutmeg

¼ tsp tarragon vinegar

Salt and pepper

4 ripe medium tomatoes

1 Fine chop the chicken. In a small pan, boil down the cream and dissolved cornstarch until very thick. Fold in the chicken, nutmeg, tarragon vinegar, and check seasoning.

2 Slice the tops off the tomatoes to make a lid. Scoop out the tomato pulp, leaving just the skin and flesh. Stuff the inside with the chicken mixture and replace the lid. Bake in the oven at 400°F for 5 minutes or until heated through. Serve as soon as possible.

Provençal tomatoes

It's the combination of flavor and texture that makes these so good. They heat up to a delicious taste, transforming a dull dish into a feast. If you serve these immediately, the crumbs will still be crisp. Later on, they soften up, although the flavor is a little better.

¼ cup olive oil and/or melted butter

2 Tbsp fresh bread crumbs

1 garlic clove, chopped fine

1 tsp chopped fresh parsley

4 medium tomatoes

Salt and pepper

1 Heat the oil and/or butter in a pan and add the bread crumbs. When they start to turn brown, lower the heat and add the garlic and parsley. Drain through a sifter when the crumbs have browned lightly.

2 Meanwhile, slice the tomatoes in half across the middle, season, and place under a broiler or in a medium oven (325°F) until soft—about 20 minutes.

3 Top with the bread crumbs and return to the oven for a further 5 minutes. Keep warm until required, or cool and reheat in a 400°F oven.

▶ Provençal tomatoes

Yorkshire puddings

Made with melted beef drippings and served with gravy, this classic accompaniment is every bit as delicious as the beef with which it is served.

1 cup milk

½ cup flour

2 eggs, beaten

½ tsp salt

¼ cup melted butter or beef drippings

1 Pour the milk into a blender, put on the lid, and switch on. With the machine still running, carefully remove the lid and add the flour and eggs alternately through the hole. Then add the salt and pour in the melted butter or drippings.

2 Turn off the blender and allow the batter to rest for at least 30 minutes. Pour into oiled muffin pans and cook in a very hot oven until the batter is risen and hollow. Remove any uncrisp batter from the middle. Serve with roasted beef.

Polenta cakes

Polenta has a good texture and neutral background flavor, making it ideal to serve with steak in a sauce, as an alternative to mashed potatoes.

8 oz ready-cooked polenta

¼ stick butter

¼ cup chopped bacon, fried crisp

3 Tbsp chopped and cooked cabbage

1 egg, beaten

1 Reheat the polenta with the butter until the butter has melted, stirring frequently, then beat in the bacon, cabbage, and egg. Do not add salt. Bake in four small, well-oiled individual muffin pans, or bake whole in a large flat dish. If you are cooking the mixture in one piece, turn out and cut into circles with a large cutter. Chill.

2 To serve, broil under a hot broiler or on a grill and crisscross with a hot skewer.

▶ Yorkshire puddings

Fried onion rings

This recipe makes very crisp, sweet rings—everything that an onion ring should be. Take care not to overbrown them; they burn and become bitter and black very easily.

1 Peel and slice the onions into thin rings and discard the centers. Sprinkle lightly with the salt and leave for 10 minutes, then rinse them well to remove the salt, and pat dry on paper towels.

2 Dust the rings liberally with the cornstarch to coat and leave for 5 minutes, then turn them over, packing the cornstarch well down onto them. Heat the oil in a deep pan until just smoking. Plunge the onion rings into the oil for a couple of minutes, lift them out, and, while the oil is reheating, sprinkle them with a teaspoonful more cornstarch.

3 Return them to the hot fat and fry them until they are really crisp but do not allow them to become very dark or they will taste bitter. Drain on paper towels and keep warm.

▶ **Follow the photographs overleaf for a full demonstration.**

2 medium onions

2 tsp fine sea salt

4 tsp cornstarch

Oil (preferably enough for deep frying)

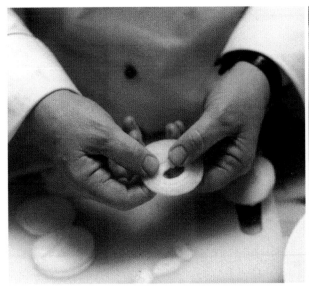

1 Sprinkle lightly with salt.

2 Pat the rinsed rings dry on paper towels.

3 Dust the rings liberally with cornstarch.

4 Plunge the rings into the hot oil for a couple of minutes.

5 Return the rings to the fat after another dusting with cornstarch.

6 Fry until they are really crisp.

7 The perfect onion rings—crisp and golden, but not too dark.

Red cabbage

Red cabbage is a good accompaniment to a plain broiled steak with horseradish sauce.

1 Soften the onion in the butter for 10 minutes with 2 tablespoonfuls of water. When the mixture has dried out and the onion begins to fry, add the caraway seeds, if using.

2 Meanwhile wash the cabbage, core, and remove the tough ribs, then fine shred it. Add it with the vinegar to the pan and with one cup of lightly salted water.

3 Cover and simmer the cabbage until cooked then remove the lid, mix in the apple and sugar, and boil off any remaining water.

1 medium onion, chopped

½ stick butter

½ tsp caraway seeds (optional)

1½ lb red cabbage

2 tsp red wine vinegar

1 eating apple, cored and cubed

1 tsp sugar

Potato pancakes

Do not cook these pancakes too far in advance—the fresher the better.

1 Place the potatoes and flour in a food processor, switch on, and feed in the eggs a little at a time. Thin out the mixture with milk if necessary, to a thick cream. Season to taste.

2 Heat a little of the butter or oil in a heavy skillet and pour in one tablespoonful of the batter at a time to form four pancakes or as many as the skillet will hold. Cook on one side and turn them over when the underside has browned. Cook the other side until the cakes puff up a little, then lift out, and keep warm. Repeat until the batter is used up.

1 lb boiled potatoes

4 Tbsp flour

5 eggs, beaten

2 Tbsp milk, if required

Salt and pepper

Butter or oil

◀ Red cabbage

Fried parsley or celery leaves

The way the flavor is concentrated when these leaves are crisply deep-fried is amazing. Don't allow them to overbrown.

1 Fry a test piece of parsley or celery leaf in the oil to check the temperature. If it is too hot, the leaves will burn before you can remove them and if it is too cool they will remain soggy.

2 Remove the stalks from a large bunch of dry, clean parsley or some celery tops. When the temperature is right, drop the leaves into the oil until the crackling noise stops, and then remove quickly with a slotted spoon. Drain on paper towels.

Glazed shallots

These are the traditional accompaniments to red wine sauces. Together with mushrooms and lardons of bacon they make up the garnish for "à la Bourguignonne."

1 Melt the butter with some water in a large pan and cook the shallots in a single layer very gently until soft. Increase the heat and brown them lightly.

2 Pour in the vinegar, add the sugar, and boil briskly until the shallots are coated with a glaze.

¼ **stick butter**

24-36 **small shallots (according to size)**

¼ **cup balsamic vinegar**

3 **Tbsp raw sugar**

Glazed shallots with red wine sauce

1 Proceed as for Glazed shallots recipe but then remove the shallots and add the red wine to the pan. Boil to reduce to ½ cup.

2 Pour in the broth, add the butter, and simmer to a fine sauce consistency. Return the shallots to the pan.

24-36 **small shallots (according to size)**

¾ **cup red wine**

⅔ **cup strong beef broth**

¼ **stick butter**

◀ Fried parsley and celery leaves

Bistro

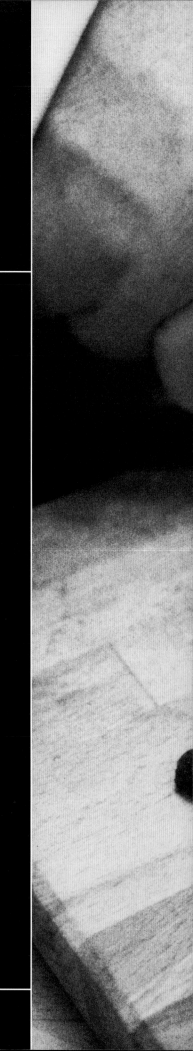

AT TIMES, COOKING NEEDS TO BE ADVENTUROUS AS

WELL AS DELICIOUS—WITHOUT BEING COMPLICATED.

HERE ARE SOME DISHES THAT YOU CAN PREPARE

QUICKLY, INCLUDING THE FAMOUS DISH OF GROUND

RAW BEEF STEAK, TARTARE (WHICH MUST BE CHILLED

BEFORE SERVING) TO SAY NOTHING OF A COUPLE OF

HAMBURGERS. THE LESS YOU HANDLE THESE, THE

BETTER THE TEXTURE.

Steak au poivre

This is just one version of this timelessly popular dish. Marinating the steak enables the pepper flavor to penetrate the meat while the cream cools its heat.

4 sirloin butt steaks weighing 7 or 8 oz each

2 tsp ground black pepper for sprinkling

2 garlic cloves, minced

½ cup cognac

2 Tbsp butter

1 tsp coarsely ground black pepper for the sauce

1 cup heavy cream

½ cup crème fraîche or sour cream

1 tsp beef glaze or broth (optional)

Salt

1 Sprinkle the pepper and garlic over one side of the steaks and press well in. Leave for 30 minutes.

2 Brush a ridged griddle pan with oil until smoking hot. Place the steaks on the ridges peppered-side down but do not press down. Turn over once during cooking.

3 Meanwhile, pour the cognac, butter, and pepper for the sauce in a large skillet and reduce to 1 tablespoon. Pour in the cream, the crème fraîche, and the beef glaze or broth, if using. Reduce to a light coating consistency, add salt to taste, and set aside.

4 When the steaks are almost done, lift them, pepper-side up, into the skillet and allow to bubble for 20 seconds. Do not submerge. Transfer the steaks to hot plates and pour the sauce around. Serve with the vegetables of your choice.

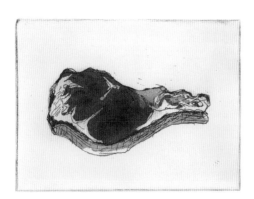

Steak au poivre 2

White peppercorns are the fully mature ones and hold real heat; black peppercorns are dried green ones and hold flavor. Mix the two together and you have the best of both worlds! Brushing the steaks with a little Dijon mustard is another way of making the peppercorns stick to the meat if the butter and oil fail to achieve this.

1 Tbsp white peppercorns

1 Tbsp black peppercorns

½ stick unsalted butter

1 Tbsp hazelnut oil

**4 top loin steaks weighing
6 oz each**

Salt

3 Tbsp cognac

1 Tbsp beef broth (page 22)

1 Crush or grind the peppercorns by hand using a pestle and mortar or spread them out on a flat board or paper and crush with a rolling pin. Melt the butter and oil together in a heavy pan, and brush the steaks with this mixture on both sides. Season with salt and then press them into the peppercorns to make them stick. Turn over and press into the rest of the peppercorns.

2 Reheat the pan and cook the steaks to your liking, turning once. Pour the cognac over them and ignite or place the steaks on individual serving plates, add the cognac to the pan, and light with a match to remove the alcohol. Add the beef glaze or broth and the remaining butter. Whisk and boil up to mix effectively. Divide among the steaks. Serve with fried potatoes.

Beef stroganoff

This has to be made with sour cream to achieve the proper flavor. Simmering the mushrooms in the wine gives the whole dish a delightful piquancy. Plain noodles are the best accompaniment.

1 Place the beef slices between 2 sheets of nonstick parchment and beat with a meat bat to thin them. Slice into 1-inch wide strips.

2 Heat the butter in a large heavy pan until it begins to brown. Quickly sauté the beef, turning it often to brown it evenly and lightly. Season, lift out, and put aside.

3 Add the onions to the butter in the pan and simmer until soft. Add the mushrooms and when they have given up most of their moisture add the paprika, nutmeg, wine. Reduce this by fast boiling to a quarter of the original amount. Add the cream and simmer to a thick coating consistency. Fold in the meat and bring to a boil again, when the sauce will thin out a little. Check the seasoning and serve with noodles.

1½ lb beef tenderloin, cut into ½-in thick slices

¾ stick butter

1 medium onion, chopped

5 cups sliced mushrooms

2 tsp paprika

2 pinches of nutmeg

¼ cup white wine

1 cup sour cream

Warm shredded beef salad

The slightly sweet dressing and the caramelized strips of beef make a mouthwatering addition to the salad, and arugula adds a touch of heat to the other crisp salad leaves.

3 Tbsp soy sauce

1 Tbsp sweet sherry

½ tsp ground mixed peppercorns

¼ tsp chili powder

1 tsp clear honey

1½ lb short loin/entrecôte steaks

Selection of salad leaves (arugula, frisée, and escarole)

1 Tbsp mirin

1 Tbsp peanut oil

1 tsp rice vinegar

1 tsp sesame oil

2 tsp peanut oil

2 tsp cornstarch

½ tsp salt

4 scallions, sliced diagonally

Sesame seeds, to garnish

1 Mix together the soy sauce, sherry, ground peppercorns, chili powder, and honey.

2 Remove all fat and gristle from the beef and shred it into thin strips; add the marinade and mix well. Allow to marinate for 30 minutes.

3 Arrange the salad on individual plates. Mix together the mirin, the 1 tablespoon peanut oil, and the rice vinegar, and dress the salad with the mixture.

4 Mix and heat the sesame oil and the 2 teaspoons peanut oil in a wok or skillet. Drain the beef and pat dry on paper towels. Sift and sprinkle over the cornstarch and the salt, and immediately tip into the hot skillet. Stir-fry until crisp or caramelized then turn out onto the salad, mix well, and scatter over the scallions. Serve warm, garnished with sesame seeds.

Italian hamburgers

This attractive, colorful dish can be prepared in advance and put under the broiler at the last minute. Serve with some hot, crusty bread sprinkled with good olive oil.

1 Dip the tomatoes briefly in boiling water and remove the skin and stalk. Halve them crosswise, remove the seeds and veins, and then cut them carefully in several places to flatten them as much as possible into 4 large round pieces. Set aside.

2 Shape the meatball mixture into 4 hamburgers and cook gently on both sides until firm. Transfer to an ovenproof dish and place the tomato pieces on top. Cover with the basil and then the mozzarella slices sprinkled with the grated cheese and crisscross the anchovy fillets over. Place under the broiler until the cheeses melt. Serve immediately.

2 large beef tomatoes

1 quantity Italian meatball mixture (below)

8 large basil leaves

4 large slices mozzarella cheese

¼ cup grated Cheddar cheese

8 anchovy fillets

Italian meatball mixture

This is a useful, basic mixture and you can add more of the Parmesan cheese to the recipe if you are not serving some separately at the table. Pancetta can be very salty, so blanch the slices and pat them dry on paper towels before you chop them. If you prefer, substitute slices of ordinary bacon.

1 Mix all the ingredients together.

2 Form into balls, hamburgers (as above) or any other preferred shape. Cook in a skillet on all sides until firm.

1 lb ground beef

1 Tbsp fresh white bread crumbs

1 Tbsp chopped onion

1 or 2 garlic cloves, minced

2 pancetta slices, chopped

1 Tbsp grated Parmesan cheese

1 egg yolk

◀ Italian hamburgers

Steak packages with tomato stuffing

The stuffing for this steak dish is a great favorite. Tarragon and steak is a well-known combination and the tomato gives an added piquancy.

1 small onion, chopped

Oil, to fry

2 garlic cloves, minced

4 tomatoes, peeled and seeded

1 Tbsp tarragon vinegar

1 tsp Dijon mustard

1 Tbsp fine chopped fresh tarragon

1 tsp sugar

4 sirloin steaks, weighing 8 oz each

Salt and pepper

1 Cook the onion in a little oil until soft. Add the other ingredients except the steaks, season, and cook to a thick purée. Add sugar to taste.

2 Make a slit in the side of each steak, working the knife first one way, then the other to create a pocket. Spoon the tomato mixture into a pastry bag and fill each steak with a tablespoonful of it. Stitch up the opening with kitchen string.

3 Preheat the oven to 375°F. Season the steaks and fry to your liking, then allow them to rest in the oven to heat the filling through. Remove the string. Serve with Potato pancakes (page 67) and any juices from the pan poured over.

Cold sliced beef

This dish may be made equally well with short loin instead of filet mignon. Roast it in the oven for 25 minutes to the pound (for rare) or 35 minutes to the pound (for well done) meat.

1 Mix the marinade ingredients into a paste and spread it over the beef. Chill overnight.

2 Pre-heat the oven to 425°F. Roast for 25 minutes for rare or 40 minutes for well done, basting often. Remove and allow to cool, turning it in its juices. Wrap up, chill, then slice fine.

3 Mix together the ingredients for the mirin dressing. Use to dress a mixed salad to serve with the beef, alongside baked potatoes or crusty bread, and a sweet chutney.

VARIATION: See Beef carpaccio page 150

MUSTARD MARINADE:

2 tsp fresh ground mixed peppercorns

¼ cup grapeseed oil

2 cloves garlic, minced

2 tsp ground ginger

3 Tbsp wholegrain mustard

1 Tbsp brown sugar

1 lb beef tenderloin

MIRIN DRESSING:

1 Tbsp mirin

1 Tbsp peanut oil

1 tsp rice vinegar

Spiedini (meat and sage kabobs)

Italians love sage and use it to flavor many different meats, especially liver. This is a favorite recipe incorporating sage. Adding a couple of pieces of calves' liver is traditional.

1 Soak four wooden skewers in water for 30 minutes. Roll a piece of bacon round each cube of steak and skewer each one followed by a piece of wiener and a sage leaf. Heat the oil in a skillet. Place the kabobs in the skillet, turning them to brown gently and evenly. Pour in the Marsala and wine or vermouth, and allow to bubble and reduce by half.

2 Add the broth, cover, and simmer for 5 minutes. Transfer the kabobs to a serving dish and boil down the juices to form a glaze. Pour over the skewers and serve on a bed of chopped spinach seasoned with nutmeg and butter.

24 slices bacon

2½ lb top sirloin butt steak cut into 24 cubes

24 sage leaves

8 wieners, each cut into 3 pieces

⅓ cup olive oil

⅔ cup Marsala

⅔ cup dry white wine or vermouth

1¼ cups beef broth

Steak sandwich

This recipe is so quick and easy that we forget how utterly delicious it is. The hot bread soaks up the wonderful mustard juices of the steak.

1 Lay the steaks on a firm surface and beat them into the shape of the bread slices with a meat bat. Season with salt and freshly ground black pepper.

2 Heat a stovetop grill pan and brush with oil. Put the bread on the bars and toast, pressing down with a metal spatula until golden. Remove from the pan and slice off the crusts. Spread the uncooked surfaces with the butter and mustard.

3 Heat a skillet, brush with oil, and add the steaks. Cook on both sides until rare, or done to your taste. Transfer to the mustard-buttered toasts and top with the second halves of toast. Trim off any excess bread and serve with a green salad.

4 fillet steaks, ½ in thick

Salt and black pepper

Peanut oil, to brush

8 slices bread from either a square or French round loaf

1 stick unsalted butter

½ cup Dijon mustard

Steak tartare

A classic dish. As the meat is uncooked, buy it on the day you plan to serve the dish and grind it yourself just before you eat it. Use fresh, free-range egg yolks. Using tenderloin steak will make a finer, textured cake.

1 lb boneless top loin or tenderloin steak

2 egg yolks (see page 4)

1 medium onion, chopped fine

2 tsp lemon juice

¼ cup olive oil

1 tsp salt

½ tsp black pepper

1 garlic clove, chopped fine

1 Tbsp chopped fresh parsley

1 Remove any fat or gristle from the meat.

2 Finely grind the steak in a food processor. Add the other ingredients and blend well. Form into 4 round cakes and chill. Serve with a salad.

Green peppercorn steaks

Green peppercorns are the same as black peppercorns if they are allowed to dry but the taste when they are moist is totally different, so this does not count as a variation of steak au poivre.

1 Mix the dried thyme with the flour. Toss the steaks in it and fry them in the butter for 3 minutes each side. Transfer to a 100°F oven.

2 Add the wine to the pan and reduce to 1 tablespoon. Add the broth, the mustard, and the cream and boil fiercely until the sauce reaches a coating consistency. Fold in the tomato concasse and stir in the green peppercorns.

3 Pour any juices that may have oozed out of the steaks into the sauce. Serve the steaks coated with the sauce. These steaks are excellent with French fries.

1 tsp dried thyme

1 Tbsp flour, seasoned

4 sirloin butt steaks

½ stick butter

¾ cup red wine

¾ cup chicken broth

1 tsp Dijon mustard

1¼ cups heavy cream

3 Tbsp tomato concasse (tomatoes that have been peeled, pipped, and cut into tiny cubes)

1 Tbsp green peppercorns, rinsed and chopped

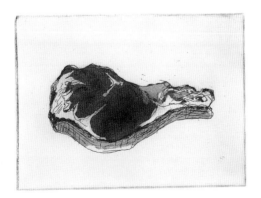

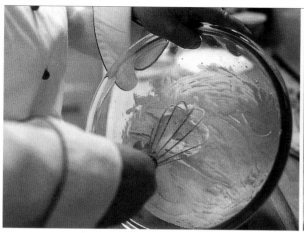 

Beef fritters

Cooking the steak inside a coating of batter always produces a juicy morsel inside. These fritters have been seasoned with chile, but for a change try adding some chopped fresh tarragon leaves to the eggs instead.

6 Tbsp flour

½ tsp salt

2 eggs, beaten

2 tsp five-spice paste

2 tsp hot curry powder

2 Tbsp fresh chopped parsley

1½ lb boneless top loin steak

1 Mix together the flour and the ½ teaspoon salt. Whisk the eggs with the paste and powder. Add the chopped parsley. Slice the steak thinly on the slant. Season with salt and pepper.

2 Coat with the flour then dip into the beaten egg mixture. Fry in oil until crisp. Turn over and cook the other side.

3 Drain on paper towels and cut into 2-inch squares. These are good with Red bell pepper sauce (see page 45).

Nasi goreng

This Indonesian fried rice dish is much loved by students as the amount of steak, shrimp, omelet, and rice can be varied according to suit individual finances. Buy shrimp with the shells on so you can make the broth.

2 eggs

6 oz raw shrimp

12 oz flank or sirloin butt steak

1 onion, chopped

2 garlic cloves, minced

¼ cup sunflower oil

4 scallions, sliced thin

2 cups cooked rice

4 tsp soy sauce

Salt and pepper

2 Tbsp dried onion flakes, roasted

½ cucumber, sliced into strips

1 Make an omelet with the 2 eggs and slice into strips. Set aside. Shell and devein the shrimp and boil the shells in water to make a fish broth. Shred the beef into thin strips.

2 In a blender blend together the onion, garlic, and strained fish broth with 1 tablespoon of the oil. Pour this into a pan or wok and reduce to a purée. Add the rest of the oil, stir in the meat and shrimp and cook until firm. Add the scallions and rice, mix together, and sprinkle with soy sauce. Season to taste with salt and pepper.

3 Turn onto a serving dish and garnish with the omelet strips, onion flakes, and cucumber.

Breaded steaks with basil

Adding dried basil to the bread crumbs provides an interesting and unusual flavor. Maître d'hôtel butter (page 48) goes very well with these steaks. Use sirloin butt steak.

1¼ cups dry bread crumbs

¼ cup dried basil

¼ tsp salt

12 thin slices frying steak

2 eggs, beaten

¼ cup oil

½ stick butter

1 lemon

Fried parsley sprigs or celery leaves (page 69)

1 Mix together the bread crumbs, dried basil, and salt. Dip the steaks first in the egg and then the bread crumb, pressing in well.

2 Heat the oil and butter together and gently fry the steaks until golden. Drain and serve each with a wedge of lemon and fried parsley or celery leaves.

New Orleans hamburgers

A traditional, satisfying recipe for hamburgers. Serve with the traditional accompaniments listed for an authentic New Orleans flavor.

1 Cook the onions in the oil until lightly browned then transfer to a large bowl. Add the beef and all the remaining ingredients. Mix thoroughly and shape into 4 wide hamburgers, ½ inch thick.

2 Heat a large skillet and cook them on both sides, flattening them as they cook. Serve on hot French bread with shredded lettuce, pickle, sliced tomato, and mayonnaise.

1 medium onion, chopped

1 Tbsp peanut oil

1 lb ground beef

1 tsp salt

½ tsp black pepper

Pinch of chili powder

¼ tsp paprika

1 tsp Worcestershire sauce

Stuffed steak packages

This is an attractive way of presenting a well-done steak. It's not difficult to make the pocket providing you have a sharp knife. Do not overfill the steak or the mixture may burst out during cooking.

1 Cook the onion in the butter until soft then add the mushrooms, parsley, and thyme and cook gently for 5 minutes. Stir in the ham and bread crumbs, season, and allow to cool.

2 Make a slit in the side of each steak, working the knife first one way, then the other to create a pocket. Divide the stuffing into 4 portions and stuff each steak with some, taking care not to overfill. Stitch up the opening with kitchen string. Fry the steaks quickly to brown them then allow them to rest in the oven at 375°F to heat the stuffing through. Remove the string. Serve cut in slices topped with a piece of your favorite flavored butter (page 48).

1 medium onion, chopped

¼ stick butter

¾ cup chopped mushrooms

1 tsp chopped parsley

1 tsp fresh thyme

6 oz ham, chopped

2 Tbsp fresh white bread crumbs

Salt and pepper

4 sirloin butt steaks, weighing 8 oz each

Grilling & Broiling

TO MY MIND, NO OTHER METHOD OF COOKING CAN

IMPROVE ON A PERFECTLY BROILED STEAK. COOK OVER

A FIERCE HEAT TO START WITH, SO THE SURFACE OF

THE MEAT BECOMES FLAVORED WITH A DELICIOUS

COATING AS THE JUICES INSIDE RISE TO THE SURFACE

AND CARAMELIZE. LOWER THE HEAT AND CONTINUE

GENTLY COOKING UNTIL THE REQUIRED DEGREE OF

DONENESS IS REACHED AND EAT IMMEDIATELY. THERE

ARE MORE CHOICES OF CUTS THAN MOST PEOPLE ARE

AWARE OF, SO THIS CHAPTER SHOWCASES SOME LESS

KNOWN ONES AS WELL AS THE OLD FAVORITES.

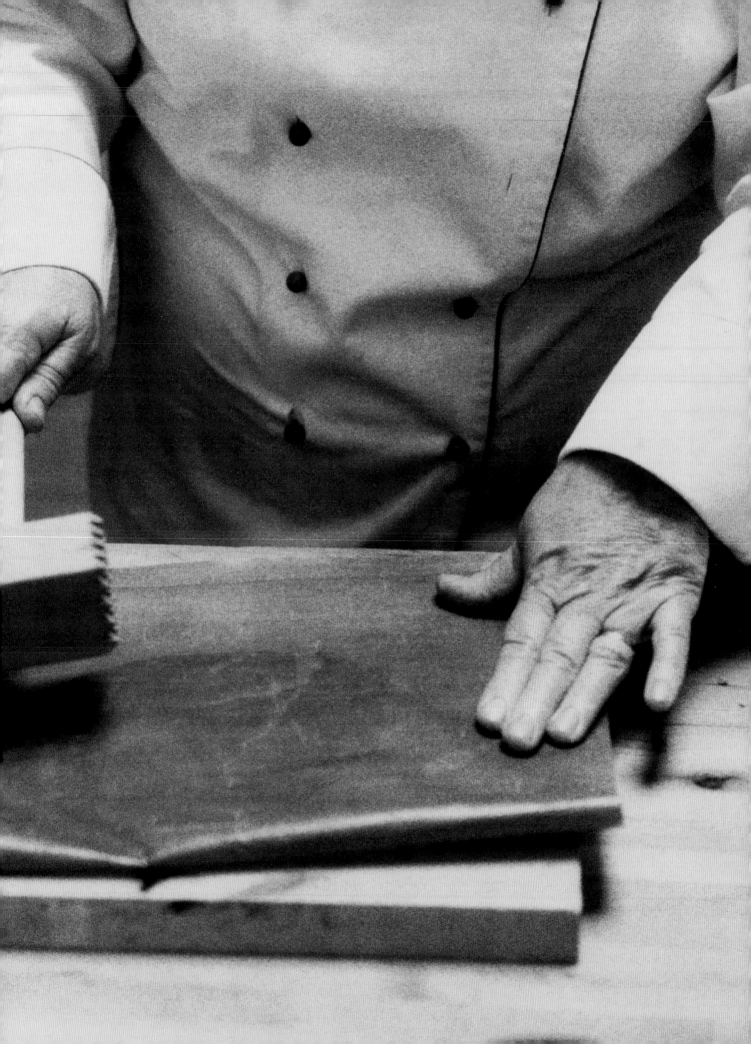

T-bone steak

To be a proper T-bone steak, the tenderloin and short loin steaks will still be attached to the bone, not served separately. This ensures that the meat is cooked "stretched." Once removed from the bone, the meat can shrink in cooking and then will have a totally different texture – quite wrong.

4 T-bone steaks

Oil

Salt and pepper

Watercress

1 Preheat the broiler or barbecue. Brush the steaks with oil and seasoning and cook for 5 minutes, lowering the temperature if the steak is developing a hard crust.

2 When beads of blood appear on the surface, turn the steak and cook to your liking – about another 4 minutes for rare or 5 for medium. Serve with a garnish of watercress and one or two flavored butters.

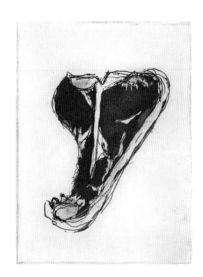

Sirloin butt steak

This muscle is either sliced across and served with its delicious crust of fat edging it, (in which case the amount is only dictated by how much you can eat!) or it is seam cut—that is, divided into separate portions within the muscle and the fat usually removed. This can be a tough cut, so, if it has not been hung to properly tenderize it, leave it in a plastic bag with 4 tablespoons oil for 3 or 4 days. Drain and wipe off excess oil before seasoning and cooking.

4 sirloin butt steaks, weighing at least 8 oz each

Salt and pepper

Oil, to brush

1 Preheat the broiler, grill or barbecue. Season and oil the steaks and cook to your liking.

2 Serve with crisp onion rings or other garnish.

Broiled steak with a mustard crust

The marinade becomes crusty as it broils, making a pungent, crisp topping. A splendid lunch dish to eat with salad and a glass of cold beer.

MUSTARD MARINADE:

¼ cup oil

2 tsp fresh ground black peppercorns

2 garlic cloves, minced

¼ cup wholegrain Dijon mustard

2 tsp brown sugar

2 tsp ground ginger

4 sirloin butt steaks, weighing 7 oz each

¼ stick butter

1 Mix the marinade ingredients together, adding a few drops of water if necessary, to form a thick paste.

2 Marinate the steaks in this mixture in a plastic bag for a couple of hours in the fridge. Remove the steaks from the bag and scrape any excess marinade back into it. Preheat the broiler.

3 In the meantime seal the steaks in the butter for 2 minutes each in a hot pan, smear over the marinade, and place under the broiler to form a crust. Transfer to warmed plates, pour over the buttery juices from the pan and serve.

► Sirloin steak

Carpetbag steak

The traditional carpetbag steak was stuffed with fresh oysters. In this version
I have substituted mushrooms, with the addition of a few dried porcini to improve
the mushroom flavor.

1 Put the porcini in a cup and cover with boiling water. Allow to soak for
20 minutes then drain, reserving the liquid. Rinse the porcini in cold
running water to remove any grit, then chop coarsely. Strain the porcini
soaking liquid through a sifter lined with paper towels to remove the grit.

2 Heat the oil in a skillet, add the garlic, and sauté until golden. Add the
mushrooms and porcini and stir-fry until they begin to brown. Add the
porcini soaking liquid, bring to a boil, and simmer until the liquid has
been absorbed. Stir in the parsley, season, then set aside to cool. Put the
steaks on a board and, using the point of a sharp knife, make a pocket in
the steak to within ¾ inch of the edges. Stuff each steak with a quarter of
the mushroom mixture. Season with salt and freshly ground black
pepper.

3 Heat a ridged griddle pan and brush with oil. Add the steaks and cook
over high heat until the surfaces are seared with ridge marks. Continue
cooking until the steaks are done to your liking. Serve with crusty bread.

1 oz dried porcini

¼ cup peanut oil

3 garlic cloves, chopped

1 lb mushrooms, sliced

**4 top loin steaks, ¾ inch thick,
well-trimmed**

¼ cup chopped fresh parsley

Salt and pepper

Chateaubriand steak (whole)

These are taken from the wide end of the tenderloin before it tapers off and divides into two parts. There are only two classical-cut steaks on each whole fillet, each weighing up to 10 oz depending on the size of the individual animal. Cooked whole, they are a magnificent sight and traditionally called "à cheval" if served broiled with two fried eggs on top, as shown here.

4 Chateaubriand steaks, weighing 8 to 10 oz each

Salt and pepper

Oil

1 Preheat the broiler or barbecue.

2 Season and oil the steaks. Broil to your liking and serve.

TIP It is very difficult to produce a hot "blue" steak because by the time the center is warm, the outside is well-done. I have found the best way around this difficulty is to broil the steak fiercely to draw flavor and juices to the surface for one or two minutes each side, then microwave the steak for 10 seconds and either serve immediately or recrisp for a further half minute under the broiler (microwave for longer if you want it well-done but juicy).

Steak Florentine-style (Bistecca alla Fiorentina)

The steaks are marinated in a very simple mixture, which gives them an intense flavor.

¼ cup olive oil

1 garlic clove, minced

1 Tbsp chopped fresh parsley

1 tsp lemon juice

Grated rind of 1 lemon

4 top loin steaks, weighing 8 oz each

Unsalted butter, to serve

1 Mix the olive oil, garlic, parsley, lemon juice, and lemon rind together and marinate the steaks in a plastic bag in this mixture for at least 2 hours.

2 Lift the steaks out of the plastic bag and shake off any surplus marinade. Broil for 3 to 5 minutes each side. Serve with a piece of unsalted butter melting on each one.

▶ Chateaubriand steak (whole)

Chateaubriand steak (butterflied)

4 Chateaubriand steaks, weighing 8 to 10 oz each

Salt and pepper

Radishes, to garnish

1 Preheat the broiler. Slice each steak around without cutting right through, until it can be opened out like a book.

2 Place between 2 nonstick baking sheets and flatten a little with a meat bat. Season and broil for 2 minutes each side for rare. Serve with a flavored butter or a sauce of your choice, garnished with radishes.

Short loin/entrecôte steaks

Rubs and marinades improve the flavor and texture of these steaks (see pages 14–17), which is moderately tender. Better-quality steak comes from nearer the head end than the tail, where the gristle goes deeper into the meat. By the time these steaks are trimmed, with a little fat left on the upper edge, they should weigh about 8 oz, so you will have to start with one weighing 10 to 11 oz untrimmed.

4 short loin/entrecôte steaks, each weighing 10 to 11 oz untrimmed

Salt and pepper

Oil

1 Preheat the broiler. Remove half the band of top fat on the steaks, discarding the line of tough gristle underneath. Remove any loose end bits, because they can be tough. You should now have a single slice of meat muscle.

2 Broil for 3½ minutes a side for a medium steak 1 inch thick and less or more if you like it rarer or more well-done.

▶ Chateaubriand steak (butterflied)

Steak with morel mushrooms

The dried morels must be soaked in water for at least 30 minutes to rehydrate them. The resulting broth is full of flavor and is added to the cream sauce. Be careful not to set light to the cognac when you add it to the pan; it's a good idea to pour it in away from the source of heat.

¾ oz dried morel mushrooms

¼ stick butter

2 Tbsp cognac

1 cup heavy cream

Salt and pepper

4 fillet steaks (tournedos), weighing 5 oz each

1 In a saucepan soak the morels in enough cold water to cover them twice over and leave for 30 minutes. Gently swirl them in the water to clean and release any grit that is clinging to them. Bring them to a boil and then strain them through cheesecloth, catching the soaking liquid in a bowl as you do so.

2 Heat the butter in the same saucepan, return the morels, and pour in the cognac. Reduce to one tablespoon, add the morel liquid, and lift the morels onto a plate. Add the cream and some salt and pepper to the pan and reduce to a light coating consistency. (You can do this far in advance.)

3 Preheat the broiler or barbecue and cook the steaks to your liking. Reheat the sauce and add the morels and the steaks, basting them to coat them. Serve on toasted French bread with the morels spooned over and around them.

Grilled rib roast

A French family asked us to lunch and grilled a whole boneless rib roast, like this, on a wood fire in the sitting-room, only starting to cook it as we were given a glass of wine to accompany the first course. It was pink inside, but deliciously charred and crisp on the outside. It was an unforgettable experience. To achieve a similar result, cook the meat over a grill in the garden. To carve, place it flat on a board and cut downward in thick slices.

1 Brush the meat lightly with oil and season well. Heat a griddle over a wood fire until very hot. (If it is hot enough this will prevent the meat from sticking.)

2 Put the meat on the griddle and allow it to char. Take care: it will flare up as the fat drips. Turn the meat over once or twice during cooking (it would take about 15 minutes), and serve it rare with Dijon mustard and a mixed salad.

3½ lb boneless rib eye roast

Oil, to brush

Salt and pepper

Roast beef tenderloin

To roast a whole tenderloin, the narrow end or tail has to be tucked underneath to produce a piece of meat of even thickness along the whole length. First, the tough chain muscle, which lies on one side of the cut, has to be eased away with a knife. Trimmed, the chain makes a delicious stew or can be ground finely to make hamburgers.

1 Preheat the oven to 400°F and baste the seasoned meat with melted butter – preferably clarified – throughout the cooking time. Allow the meat to rest when it is removed from the oven for about 10 minutes to let the juices redisperse throughout it. A meat thermometer inserted should register 120–125°F for rare. This will take 25 to 30 minutes. For medium-rare meat, the thermometer should register 140°F.

2 Cut into thick slices to serve. Traditionally, this is served with Sauce béarnaise (see page 36).

1 whole tenderloin

Butter for basting

Salt and pepper

108

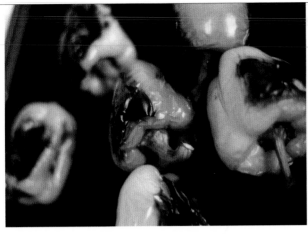

Stuffed and rolled rib eye roast

This is a flavorful cut. It must be carefully trimmed to make sure that all gristle and connecting tissue has been discarded. As the steak is seam cut, there is no top fat on this piece of muscle. In this recipe, the flavor of the bell peppers permeates the whole joint in an elusive way.

1 Untie the joint if rolled with string, remove the top flap of tough muscle, and set this aside for other uses (or buy the joint without this piece). Cut the bell peppers into 8 pieces each, discarding seeds and core. Blanch the bell peppers in boiling water for 5 minutes, drain, and pat dry with paper towels (or microwave each prepared pepper for 1 minute).

2 Heat a ridged griddle pan and char the bell pepper on both sides. Make two long pocket-like slits through the roast and rub with oil and salt to season. Stuff these cavities with the bell pepper slices, garlic, rosemary, and bay leaves. Tie 3 pieces of string round the joint and wrap it in foil. Place the peppered meat in a roasting pan with the broth or water. Roast in a high oven (450°F) for 1 hour then remove the foil.

3 Continue to roast for a further half hour for medium-done or 1 more hour for well-done, adding more water as necessary during cooking. Allow to rest for 10 minutes, remove the string, and place on a serving dish. Pour off the gravy, reduce it to strengthen the flavor if necessary, and season. Cut into 4 thick slices and serve or carve as required. Accompaniments should be roasted or sauté potatoes and a green vegetable.

1 red bell pepper

1 orange or yellow bell pepper

3 garlic cloves, peeled and cut in half

1 rosemary sprig

3 or 4 bay leaves

Salt and pepper

Boned rib eye roast about 5 in long

Oil, for rubbing

Hanging tender, hanging tenderloin, or hanger steak

This is a steak not often found. The meat, which is exceptionally juicy, has a dark color and an almost striplike appearance. Do not be put off by this; the unprepossessing exterior hides a sublime flavor. Refer to its description on page 7 for how to obtain it. Each lobe of steak will weigh 10 oz trimmed.

4 back roll steaks or 2 whole muscles, weighing 10 oz each

Salt and pepper

Oil, to brush

Lemon rind, to garnish

1 Preheat the broiler or barbecue. If the steak has not been prepared, remove all fat and sinew and rinse it well. Pat dry with paper towels. Remove the center sheet of gristle (see page 7) and divide the muscle into two individual lobes.

2 Brush the steaks with some oil and season. Place them under the broiler or the barbecue, turning them frequently, so they cook evenly all round. This will take about 10 minutes. Lift out and carve into slices against the grain. Do not overcook or they will become tough. Serve with a salad or vegetable of your choice.

Asian Dishes

THE COMBINATION OF SPICES IN ASIAN COOKING

CREATES A UNIQUE STYLE OF FLAVORING. THESE

DISHES ALWAYS INCLUDE AN INGREDIENT WITH A

CHARACTERISTIC PIQUANCY SUCH AS GINGER, SOY

SAUCE, OR TAMARIND. WHEN HOT CHILES FEATURE—

USUALLY SERVED AS A SIDE DISH—YOGURT PROVIDES

A COOLING ANTIDOTE. OIL IS THE COOKING MEDIUM,

NOT BUTTER.

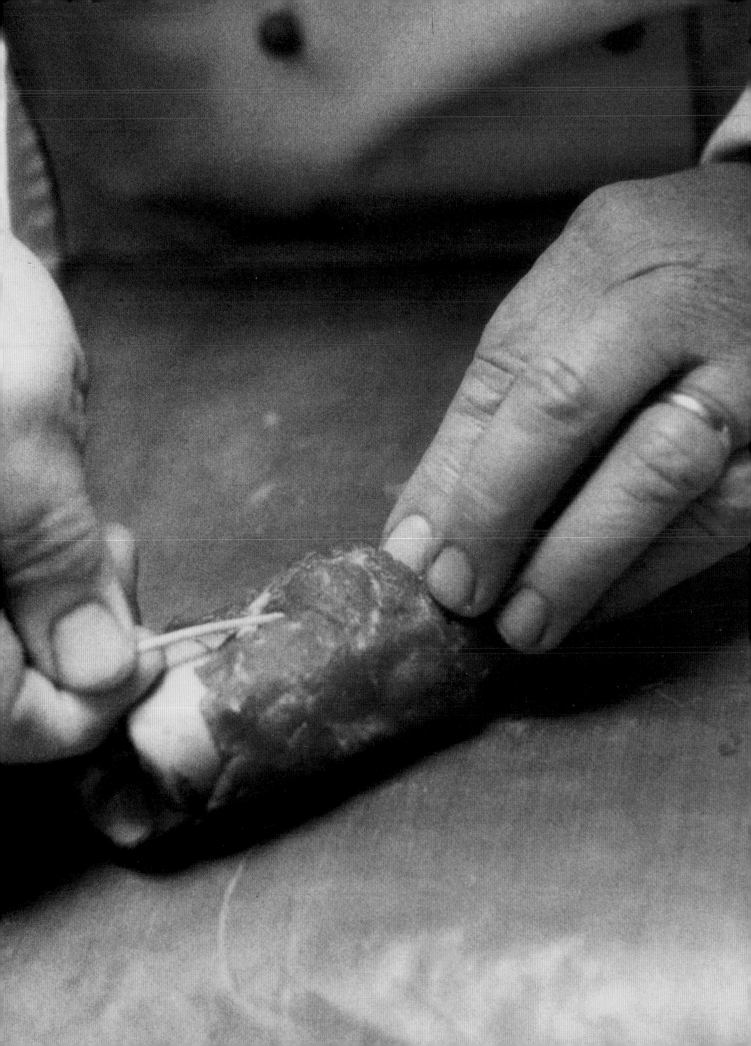

Spiced ground beef and lentil cutlets

Vary the quantity of chiles to suit your taste. If you find that your mixture is too soft to form cutlets, don't worry; use a spoon to drop it into the pan and it will thicken as it cooks.

⅔ cup red lentils

1 lb 2 oz ground beef

1 medium onion, chopped

2 green chiles, sliced

2-in piece fresh ginger root, peeled and sliced

3 bay leaves

4 cloves

8 black peppercorns

¼ tsp cardamom seeds or 6 pods

½ tsp coriander seeds

2-in stick cinnamon

1 tsp salt or to taste

1 tsp chopped fresh cilantro

2 egg yolks

GARNISH:

Sliced tomatoes, onion rings, cream coconut shavings, fresh cilantro leaves

1 In a nonstick pan cook the lentils in plenty of water for 40 minutes and then dry them out to a paste by stirring constantly to prevent them from burning on the base of the pan. Allow to cool.

2 In a saucepan mix the beef with the onions, chiles, ginger, bay leaves, cloves, peppercorns, cardamom, and coriander seeds, cinnamon, and salt in 2¼ cups water. Season and simmer for 40 minutes until dry but do not allow to brown. Cool a little then blend to a purée in a food processor. Add the lentils, cilantro, and egg yolks and blend again for a further 30 seconds to a smooth thick paste. Check the seasoning and chill.

3 Form the mixture into cutlets and fry in a little hot oil until brown on both sides. Serve garnished with sliced tomatoes, raw onion rings, shavings of creamed coconut, and fresh cilantro leaves.

Caribbean steaks

The colors in this dish are wonderful. Apple bananas are only about three inches long and very sweet. The sauce should be sweet as well, but if you want it less so, omit the sugar. Give yourself time to arrange the fruit and sweet potato onto hot plates before you start cooking the steaks, because the latter should only take about three or four minutes a side, according to how well you like them done.

MARINADE:

2 garlic cloves, minced

1 Tbsp balsamic vinegar

⅓ cup dark rum

½ tsp sugar (optional)

4 top loin steaks

Oil, to fry the fruit

12 slices ripe mango

8 slices ripe pawpaw

4 apple bananas (or large ones cut to size)

12 rounds sweet potato

¼ stick butter

1 Combine the marinade ingredients and leave the steaks in the mixture for 1 to 2 hours. Drain and pat dry on paper towels. Reserve the marinade.

2 Fry the mango, pawpaw, and banana in a little oil until they begin to brown, drain, and keep warm until needed. Do the same with the sweet potato rounds. Just before it is time to cook the steaks, arrange the fruit and sweet potato on warmed plates.

3 Melt half the butter in a heavy pan. Season the steaks and brown quickly on both sides. Keeping the heat high, baste the meat with the marinade, one tablespoonful at a time, turning the steaks over to coat them evenly. Finally, allow the marinade to form a thick, syrupy sauce and blend in the rest of the butter. Serve the steaks with the sauce spooned around.

Nargisi kabat (Eggs in meatballs)

This is a dish to take on a picnic, because it is as good cold as it is hot and it's very filling as well. It's a Sunday supper dish when served hot with a vegetable curry or a green salad.

1 In a saucepan mix 12 oz of the beef with the chiles, onion, garlic, ginger, turmeric, bay leaves, and lentils, cover with water, and simmer until all the water has evaporated, the lentils are cooked, and the meat tender (about 45 minutes). Discard the bay leaves and transfer the mixture to a food processor. Add the remaining beef and blend well.

2 Divide the mixture into 6 balls, tucking a hard-cooked egg inside each and molding the meat mixture around. Dip in the egg white and fry in hot oil. Sprinkle with chopped cilantro. Serve with a green salad or in a curried vegetable sauce.

1 lb 2 oz ground beef

2 chiles, chopped

1 onion, chopped

2 garlic cloves, minced

1 tsp grated fresh ginger root

1 tsp ground turmeric

2 bay leaves

3 Tbsp red lentils

6 small hard-cooked eggs, shelled

1 egg white

Chopped fresh cilantro, to serve

Korean steak tartare

Buy the best-quality steak and use it the same day. Korean pear slices are sold in Asian foodstores and make an interesting contrast to the meat.

1 Trim the meat of all fat and gristle. Slice it very thinly across the grain and then cut these slices into julienne strips. Mix together the marinade ingredients and add to the meat. Form into a ball and chill for 2 hours.

2 Sprinkle with shredded scallions, and roasted sesame seeds and cut into 4 portions at the table. Accompany with Korean pear slices.

1 lb sirloin butt steak

MARINADE:

¼ cup soy sauce

1 Tbsp sesame oil

2 garlic cloves, minced

1 Tbsp sugar

1 Tbsp rice wine

2–3 scallions, shredded

1 Tbsp roasted sesame seeds

Black pepper

Japanese-style beef kabobs

Beef is prized in Japan. The cattle are specially raised, fed with the finest fodder, cosseted, brushed, and massaged every day to ensure the meat is tender. The Hibachi barbecue grill is a wonderful Japanese invention and perfect for modern living. The barbecue pan, which measures approximately 11½ x 8½ in, is filled with coals, and a cast-iron barbecue rack, with a thick wooden handle, is fitted over the top. No Hibachi? Use an ordinary barbecue or broiler instead. Thread the beef onto bamboo skewers that have been soaked in water for at least 30 minutes.

MARINADE:

¼ cup grated fresh ginger root

4 garlic cloves, minced

¼ cup clear honey

¼ cup peanut oil

¼ cup light soy sauce

1 lb 2 oz fillet steak

1 Blend the ginger and garlic to a purée in a blender. Add the honey and blend again. Add the peanut oil and soy sauce and blend again. Transfer to a nonreactive shallow dish.

2 Cut the beef into ½-in cubes and add to the marinade, turning well to coat. Cover and chill overnight to develop the flavors.

3 When ready to cook, drain the meat and reserve the marinade. Thread the beef cubes onto soaked wooden skewers, 5 to 6 per skewer.

4 Heat a Hibachi, barbecue, or broiler until very hot, then cook the skewers over high heat, turning them once, for about 2 minutes each side. Brush the meat with the reserved marinade from time to time. Serve with rice-noodles, and a selection of other barbecued dishes.

Korean hamburgers

These are spiced hamburgers with a fresh flavor. The sesame oil is essential to give the dish its Korean authenticity, as is the dipping sauce.

1 lb ground beef

3 scallions, chopped fine

½-inch piece fresh ginger root, peeled and chopped

1 or 2 chiles, chopped fine

1 tsp soy sauce

1 Tbsp flour

1 egg, beaten

1 Mix all the ingredients together in a bowl and form into hamburger shapes with your hands.

2 Fry or broil on both sides according to taste. Serve with Chojang dipping sauce.

Chojang vinegar dipping sauce

SAUCE BASE:

3 Tbsp soy sauce

1 Tbsp rice vinegar

1 tsp sesame oil

1 tsp sugar

1 tsp toasted sesame seeds

Mix all the ingredients together and stir well. You may add any of the following flavorings to suit your taste: 1 tsp chopped fresh garlic and/or 1 tsp chopped fresh ginger and/or 1 tsp chopped fresh red chile, 1 Tbsp chopped fresh cilantro, and 1 Tbsp chopped scallions.

Curried ste[a]k ... [cucu]mber and banana raita

A class of 12-year[...] [...]ur of these steaks between them in less than two minutes. The less[...] [...] yogurt to tenderize and flavor meat.

1 Make up the curri[...] [...] together the onion, garlic, chile, coriander, lem[...] [...]mon, and oil. Season with black pepper. Add t[...] [...] Spread the marinade mixture over the steaks and [...] [...].

2 Make the raita b[...] [...]edients in a small bowl.

3 Heat the broiler [...] [...]5 minutes on each side, turning them once [...] [...]er and banana raita.

MARINADE:

¼ cup chopped onion

2 garlic cloves, minced

1 green chile, chopped fine

1 Tbsp ground coriander

1 Tbsp lemon juice

2 tsp paprika

½ tsp cinnamon

3 Tbsp oil

Black pepper

½ cup plain yogurt

RAITA:

2 tsp chopped fresh mint

½ cup plain yogurt

½ cucumber, diced

½ banana, sliced

4 large top loin steaks

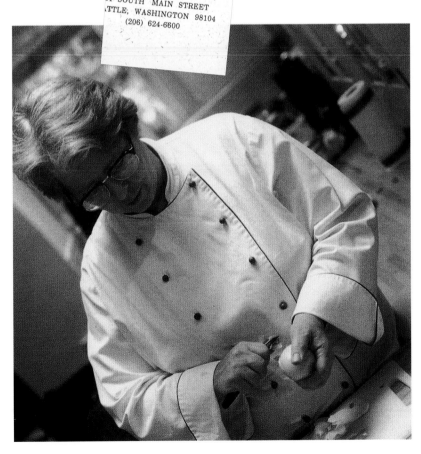

Chinese beef rolls

These delicately spiced beef rolls can be made more substantial by dipping them in beaten egg then coating them in bread crumbs. Char Sui is a marinated and cooked form of pork, which is crimson on the outside.

1 Beat out the steak thinly to at least 6 inches in diameter with a meat bat. Lay the cheese slices on it, leaving a border of meat around. Cover these with the Char Sui slices and a smear of crushed ginger. Roll up into a sausage, and secure with wooden toothpicks.

2 Melt the butter in a hot pan and gently brown the meat on all sides taking at least 8 minutes to do so. The cheese must melt and the rolls cook right through. Remove the toothpicks and serve with rice noodles, garnished with chopped scallions, red chile and cilantro leaves.

▶ Follow the photographs overleaf for a full demonstration.

4 fillet steaks, weighing 2 oz each

4 oz Edam cheese, sliced fine

2 oz Char Sui pork in wafer-thin slices

1-in piece fresh ginger root, peeled and grated

¼ stick butter

1 Add a smear of crushed grated ginger root to the char sui slices.

2 Roll up into sausages.

3 Secure with a wooden toothpick if necessary.

4 Gently brown the meat evenly on all sides.

5 After at least 8 minutes, the cheese will be melted and the rolls cooked right through.

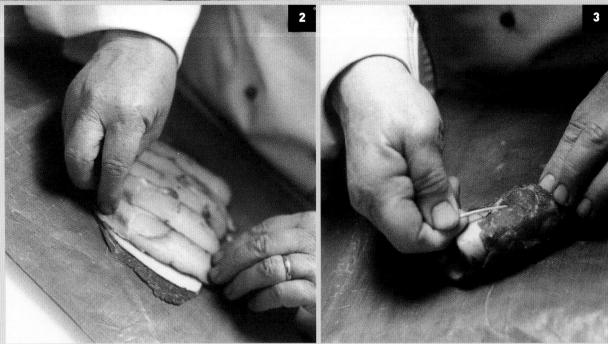

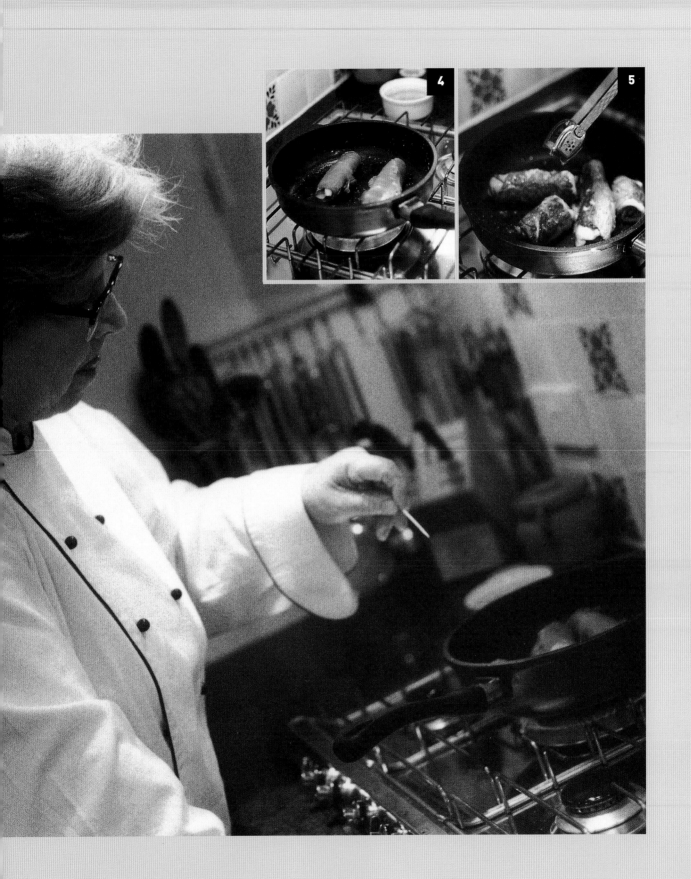

Chinese coconut meatballs

I love the delicate flavor of this dish and the sauce which is jeweled with color. If you have no skewers just form the mixture into patties, fry them in a pan, and add them to the sauce. They won't break up.

COCONUT SAUCE:

1¼ cups coconut milk

2 oz creamed coconut

1 red and 1 green chile, sliced

1 tsp chopped fresh parsley

1 scallion, chopped

1 lb 2 oz ground beef

2 tsp chopped fresh cilantro or parsley

1 garlic clove, minced

1 tsp grated fresh ginger root

2 scallions, chopped

¼ cup coconut milk

2 Tbsp fresh bread crumbs

½ tsp salt

2 Tbsp shredded coconut

1 Tbsp oil, to brush

1 Tbsp sesame seeds

1 For the sauce, heat the coconut milk in a pan together with the creamed coconut to achieve a smooth paste. Add the other sauce ingredients and seasoning, and simmer to thicken a little.

2 Preheat the oven to 225°F or the broiler. Mix together the ground beef, cilantro or parsley, garlic, ginger, scallions, coconut milk, bread crumbs, and salt. Divide into 32 pieces and roll in shredded coconut into firm balls.

3 Thread 8 balls on each skewer, brush with a little oil, scatter with sesame seeds, and bake or broil for 10 minutes, turning them over a couple of times. When the meat is just done but not hard, lay the skewers in the hot coconut sauce and baste.

4 Serve the meatballs with sliced cucumber and Chinese plum sauce.

Malay steak with coconut-peanut sauce

This peanut coating gives the steaks a wonderfully crisp texture in addition to a satisfyingly authentic taste.

SAUCE:

3 Tbsp peanut oil

1 onion, chopped

1 garlic clove, minced

Small pinch of dried chile flakes

1 tsp sugar

⅓ cup crunchy peanut butter

1 Tbsp soy sauce

¼ cup coconut milk

Peanut oil, to brush

4 top loin steaks, weighing 9 oz each

1 For the sauce, heat the oil in a small pan, add the onion and garlic, and cook until softened but not colored. Add the chile flakes, sugar, peanut butter, soy sauce, and ⅔ cup water, bring to a boil, and simmer for 5 minutes. Add the coconut milk and simmer for 1 minute. Cool.

2 When the sauce is cool, heat a skillet and brush with peanut oil. Dip the steaks into the sauce, then fry over medium heat to taste.

3 Increase the heat to crisp the surfaces for about 1 minute on each side, then serve with your choice of vegetables or salads.

European Dishes

FINE CUISINE ORIGINATED IN EUROPE. A CLASSICAL

TECHNIQUE EVENTUALLY DEVELOPED, WITH A SET OF

SPECIFIC RULES TO BE FOLLOWED. THESE TRADITIONS

HAVE SURVIVED TO THIS DAY. THE CLIMATE OF

EACH INDIVIDUAL COUNTRY, TOGETHER WITH THE

INGREDIENTS AVAILABLE, PLAYS A LARGE PART IN

DETERMINING THE STYLE OF ITS CUISINE. THE USE

OF CORN, OILS, GARLIC, AND WINE IN ANY ONE AREA,

FOR EXAMPLE, CAN GIVE WAY TO BUTTER, CREAM,

WHEAT FLOUR, AND BEER IN ANOTHER.

Pan-fried steak with Marsala and chiles

If you have no Marsala use sweet sherry or Madeira instead. The alcohol should be a little on the sweet side, to cool the chiles.

¼ cup olive oil

2 garlic cloves, minced

Salt and pepper

¾-in thick sirloin butt steaks, weighing 12 oz each

½ cup Marsala

½ cup red wine

½ cup beef broth or water

1 Tbsp tomato paste

¼ tsp crushed chiles

2 Tbsp chopped fresh parsley

1 Heat the oil and garlic in a heavy skillet until the garlic turns light brown. Lower the heat to prevent the garlic from burning, add the seasoned steaks and cook them for about 3 minutes each side.

2 Remove the steaks and keep them warm. Deglaze the pan with the Marsala and red wine and reduce until syrupy, add the broth or water, tomato paste and chili and whisk together until smooth.

3 Reduce the sauce again until a coating consistency is reached. Season. Return the steaks to the skillet with any juices that may have oozed out of the meat and baste them with the sauce. Sprinkle with parsley and serve immediately with the vegetable of your choice.

Boeuf en croûte

Also called Beef Wellington, if you include some pâté in the filling. Whatever you use, make sure that the stuffing is not wet. Plenty of juice will come out of the meat while it is cooking and keep the dish moist, but too much liquid will cause the pastry to burst open as the steam tries to escape.

¼ stick butter

1¼ lb center portion beef tenderloin, well trimmed

Salt and pepper

3 cups sliced mushrooms

¼ cup port

12 oz puff pastry

Beaten egg, to glaze

1¼ cups Grand Veneur Sauce (page 141)

1 Preheat the oven to 450°F. Heat the butter in a large pan until it begins to turn color then lay the whole piece of tenderloin in it. Turn the meat so it browns evenly all over, seasoning with salt and pepper as you do so. Transfer the meat to a plate. Cook the mushrooms in the same pan, until their moisture is released. When they are dry pour in the port and reduce it until little pools of butter begin to show. Allow to cool.

2 Roll out an oblong of puff pastry. Place the meat 1 inch in from the front edge, and top with the mushrooms. Press the flap of pastry onto the meat and brush the outside with beaten egg. Roll up the fillet as tightly as possible. Press the pastry edges together to close the parcel, removing excess pastry but leaving enough to tuck the ends around and under. Brush the parcel all over with beaten egg.

3 Pierce a couple of air holes in the pastry, decorate with any pieces that are left over, and carefully transfer to a baking sheet.

4 Cook for 20 minutes for rare, 25 minutes for medium, and 30 minutes for well-done. To serve, cut off both ends of pastry to reveal the meat, which will have shrunk a little. Divide into thick rounds, lay these flat, and serve with the sauce.

Parma ham tournedos

Tying a ribbon of Parma ham around the steak instead of the customary pieces of pork fat gives the meat a delightful Italian flavor. When set on a bed of fried bread, spinach, and ricotta, it also demands a glass of Chianti.

1 package spinach

¼ tsp grated nutmeg

Salt and pepper

½ cup ricotta cheese

4 slices crusty bread

Butter or olive oil, to fry

4 halves Provençal Tomatoes (see page 58)

4 slices Parma ham

4 filet mignon steaks weighing 4 oz each

1 Cook the spinach in boiling water, drain well, pressing out excess water, and mix with the nutmeg, seasoning, and ricotta.

2 Cut out rounds of bread and fry in the butter or olive oil. Pile a deep layer of the spinach mixture on top. Set aside in a warm place with the tomatoes.

3 Cut the Parma ham into strips the same width as the steaks and wind them firmly around the steaks. Season the meat and broil or pan-fry to your liking. Place on top of the spinach and top with the tomatoes. Serve with boiled waxy potatoes.

Steak bordelaise

Some people only drink red wine with red meat so use red to make the sauce if that is your preference. Personally, I like to make the sauce with white wine.

1 Seal 3 or 4 slices of the beef at a time for a few seconds on each side in a very hot pan. Lift them out and keep warm.

2 Continue in the same manner until they are all done, then return all the meat to the pan. Add the Bordelaise sauce (see opposite) and bubble for 5 seconds. Divide among serving plates and pour over the sauce. Garnish with the parsley.

12 ¼-in rib steak (entrecôte) slices or slices of cold rib roast

Chopped fresh parsley, to garnish

Bordelaise sauce

A sauce that reminds you of the flavor of wine but is rendered gentle with the sweetness of cooked onion.

1 Simmer the onion in two-thirds of the butter with 2 tablespoons water until the water has evaporated and the onion starts to fry. Do not allow it to brown. Add the wine and boil to reduce by at least two-thirds.

2 Add the broth and the rest of the butter and bring to a boil. Simmer until the butter emulsifies then add the parsley. Mix well, season to taste, and set aside.

¾ **stick unsalted butter**

¼ **cup sweet onion or shallot, chopped fine**

⅔ **cup white wine**

2 Tbsp chopped fresh parsley

⅔ **cup light beef broth**

Salt and pepper

Steak with wild mushrooms

Avoid washing the wild mushrooms. They are such delicate fungi that they lose flavor and character if they become water-laden. It is best to brush them clean gently with a pastry brush. The onions in their sauce provide an excellent foil for this dish.

4 2-in-thick fillet steaks, weighing 6 to 8 oz each

1¼ sticks unsalted butter

1 shallot, chopped

1 cup red wine

1 cup beef consommé

½ Tbsp cornstarch

4 oz fresh wild mushrooms (preferably girolles), cleaned and trimmed

Salt and pepper

12 Baby onions and Sauce soubise (page 57), to garnish

1 Preheat the oven to 450°F. Brown the fillets over very high heat in a skillet or chargrill them for 2 minutes on both sides. Place them in a roasting pan and cook in the oven for 5 minutes. Allow to rest in a warm place until you are ready to serve.

2 Meanwhile, melt ½ stick butter in a pan, add the shallots and wine, and boil fiercely until the shallots have absorbed the wine. Pour in the consommé and simmer for 5 minutes. Mix the cornstarch with a little water and add to the pan. Stir well and bring to a boil again to allow the sauce to thicken.

3 In a sauté pan gently fry the wild mushrooms in the remaining butter, season, and lift out. To remove the pieces of shallot, strain the sauce into the pan, mix well, and season as necessary.

4 Return the steaks to the skillet or grill to reheat and pour any juices that have oozed out of them into the sauce. Turn them and cook for a further 30 seconds on the other side and then slice them in half across and arrange each one with the cut side uppermost on a hot plate. To serve, pour the sauce around, arrange the mushrooms attractively, and garnish with the Baby onions in sauce soubise.

Steak Grand Veneur

Marinating the steaks gives them a gamey effect, which will go very well with this sauce.

1 Marinate the steaks overnight in the cold cooked marinade, then drain them and pat dry with paper towels.

2 In a heavy skillet cook the steaks to your liking in the butter. Warm the cognac in a small pan and set it alight with a match. Pour it quickly over the steaks, shake the skillet and when the flames have died out, pour the Grand Veneur sauce in and mix well to incorporate all the steak juices and cognac.

3 Transfer the steaks to individual plates, coat them with the sauce, and serve with the pine nuts sprinkled over.

4 10 oz sirloin butt steaks

1 recipe Cooked marinade, using red wine (page 14)

½ stick butter

¼ cup cognac

1 Tbsp pine nuts, browned in butter, to garnish

Sauce Grand Veneur (see below)

Sauce Grand Veneur

1 Boil together the wine, onion, thyme, and oil until the red wine has almost evaporated. Add a generous ½ cup cold water and the Espagnole sauce. Stir well and simmer for 5 minutes and then strain the sauce into a clean pan.

2 Add the fresh black pepper, Worcestershire sauce, and thyme, and reduce to required strength and consistency. Adjust the seasoning to taste.

1 cup red wine

1 small onion, chopped

1 Tbsp vegetable oil

1 cup Espagnole sauce (page 47)

1 tsp coarse ground black pepper

A few drops of Worcestershire Sauce

1 tsp dried thyme

Salt and pepper

Roast beef tenderloin with zucchini

Cooked in this way, the tenderloin will still be rare but the juices will spread back evenly through the meat resulting in a smooth pink color all over except for the outside crust. The sauce makes this a sophisticated dish.

3 lb center piece of beef tenderloin

1 recipe Cooked marinade (page 14)

½ stick butter

4 zucchini, cut into strips with a vegetable peeler

1 cup sliced mushrooms

Salt and pepper

1 Tbsp red-currant jelly

2 tsp tomato paste

14-oz can beef consommé

1 Tbsp cornstarch

1 Trim the fillet of all sinews and marinate it overnight. The next day drain and pat dry on paper towels. Reserve the marinade.

2 Put the butter in a heavy pan and heat until it starts to brown. Gently fry first the zucchini strips, drain them and set aside, and then, separately, the mushrooms. Drain and set aside. Season the meat and place in the pan, turning it so it browns evenly all over, seasoning it generously with freshly ground black pepper as you do so. This should take about 10 minutes. Place the meat in a warm oven (225°F) to rest and finish cooking.

3 Meanwhile, strain the marinade into the pan and reduce it to 1 to 2 tablespoons. Add the jelly and tomato paste and stir until dissolved completely into the sauce. Pour in the consommé. Mix the cornstarch with a little water and add to the pan to thicken the consommé.

4 Bring to a boil, add the mushrooms, and simmer gently for 1 to 2 minutes. Check the seasoning and reheat the zucchini slices. Place the steak on a serving dish, pouring any residual juices into the sauce, garnish with the zucchini strips, and carve into thick slices at table. Serve the sauce separately.

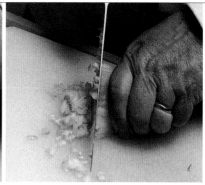

Chargrilled fillet steak with salsa verde

Salsa verde goes well with many chargrilled dishes, but here it is at its best with steak on a round of well-flavored, crisp toast. This is a perfect dinner-party or barbecue dish—make sure you serve it with plenty of sauce.

1 medium onion, peeled and chopped

¼ cup oil

3 Tbsp red wine

4 tsp cognac

2 Tbsp chopped fine mushrooms

2 Tbsp ground ham

2 tsp chopped fresh marjoram

2 tsp chopped fresh thyme

2 tsp chopped fresh parsley

4 bread slices, cut into rounds

¼ cup clarified butter

4 fillet steaks, weighing 6 oz each

Salsa verde, to serve (page 148)

1 Cook the onion in the oil, wine, and cognac until soft, add the mushrooms and continue to cook until the mixture dries out and begins to fry. Add the ham and herbs and mix well. Season (but take care, because the ham may be salty).

2 Fry the bread rounds in the butter, drain on paper towels and spread generously with the mushroom and ham mixture. Keep warm.

3 Chargrill the fillet steaks to your liking and serve on the toasted bread with the Salsa Verde spooned on top.

▶ Follow the photographs overleaf for a full demonstration.

1 & 2 Cook the onion in the oil, wine, and cognac until soft.

3 Chop the mushrooms fine.

4 Add the mushrooms and cook until mixture begins to fry.

5 Fry the bread rounds in the butter.

6 Chargrill the steaks to your liking.

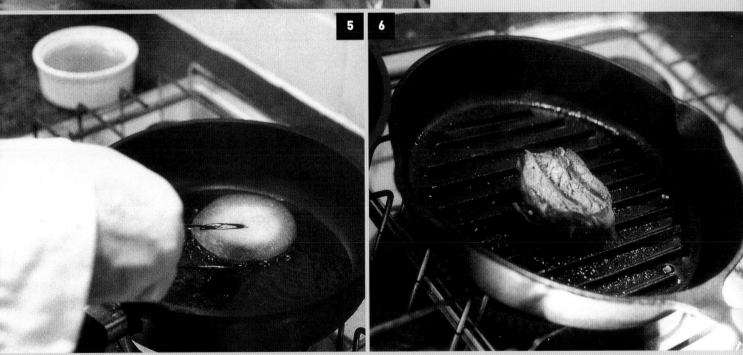

Salsa verde

This is just one version of a herby green sauce with a bit of a surprise kick in its tail.
Vary the quantities of the ingredients to suit your personal taste.

2 garlic cloves, minced

¼ cup chopped fresh parsley

¼ cup chopped fresh basil

**2 Tbsp capers in brine, drained
and chopped**

1 Tbsp Dijon mustard

½ cup olive oil

2 tsp vinegar

¼ tsp salt

1 Mix all the ingredients together
by hand or, if you prefer a
smoother texture, in a blender.

2 Serve cold to accompany the
steak of your choice.

Braised tenderloin with foie gras stuffing

A perfect dish for a special occasion. Serve it with some potato croquettes or mashed potato to mop up the sauce.

1 Combine the ingredients for the marinade and marinate the beef overnight in the mixture.

2 Blend all the stuffing ingredients together and mix well. Set aside.

3 In a hot pan quickly sear the meat on all sides in a little clarified butter. Allow to cool.

4 Slit the tenderloin down its length to within ½ inch of the sides to make a pocket. Season and insert the stuffing. Lay a few strips of pork fat lengthwise over the meat and secure with string, making sure that one strip covers the slit, and bind the meat in several places. Place in a casserole, fitting it as tightly as possible.

5 Pour the broth into a pan, add the marinade, and bring to a boil. Season and pour over the meat.

6 Preheat the oven to 350°F. Cover and braise gently in the oven for 45 minutes. Lift the meat out onto a plate, discarding the string and pork fat.

7 Reduce the meat juices to about 2 cups, blend in the cornstarch mixed with a little water, bring to a boil, check the seasoning, and add any juices from the dish on which the beef was resting. Coat the meat with the sauce and serve the rest separately. Serve with baby carrots and braised Belgian endives.

MARINADE:

1¼ cups dry white wine

6 Tbsp Madeira

1 Tbsp cognac

1 tsp salt

¼ tsp dried thyme

¼ tsp dried basil

3 parsley stalks

¼ cup chopped scallions

Truffle juice (optional)

STUFFING:

3 oz foie gras

1 tsp Madeira

1 tsp cognac

Thyme

Allspice

Pepper

2 lb beef tenderloin

Clarified butter to sear the meat

3–5 thin strips of pork fat

3¾ cups beef broth

1½ Tbsp cornstarch

Beef carpaccio

The beef has to be really cold so that it can be sliced paper-thin. It warms very quickly on the salad, which needs to have been dressed only a few moments previously.

1 quantity Mustard marinade (see page 14)

1 lb beef tenderloin

1 Tbsp oil

1 tsp salt

Arugula and Parmesan, to serve

1 Marinate the steak in mustard marinade.

2 Dress with oil and salt, then chargrill the fillet for 5 minutes, turning it often. Drop it into a bowl of iced water for 2 seconds. Lift out and pat dry on paper towels. Chill until very firm. Slice thin and serve immediately on a bed of arugula with shavings of Parmesan cheese on top.

Fillet steak with paprika and olives

The paprika colors the sauce a delicate and delicious pink, which matches the flavor.

¼ stick butter

1 tsp oil

10 pimento-stuffed green olives

1 tsp paprika

¼ roasted red bell pepper in brine

4 fillet steaks 1 inch thick

4 Tbsp white vermouth

¾ cup heavy cream

Salt and pepper

1 Melt the butter with the oil in a heavy pan. Stir in the olives and paprika. Increase the heat and, when the butter begins to brown, add the steaks and brown both sides quickly.

2 Pour in the vermouth, allow it to bubble, and reduce to 1 tablespoon. Add the cream and the roasted bell pepper, season, and bring to a boil. Transfer the steaks to individual serving plates and pour the sauce over them.

▶ Beef carpaccio

Beef piccata

The meat in this traditional Italian dish should be sliced very small and thin (hence its name) and cooked quickly, or the slices will toughen up. Return them to the sauce at the last moment.

1 red bell pepper, sliced in fine strips

1 medium onion, chopped fine

2 garlic cloves, minced

¼ stick butter

1½ lb fillet steaks, sliced thin

Flour, to dust

½ cup cognac

¼ cup white wine

1 tsp tomato paste

¼ cup heavy cream

⅔ cup chicken broth

Bell peppers, to garnish

1 Blanch the red bell pepper in boiling salted water for 2 minutes. Drain.

2 In a heavy pan gently cook the onion and the garlic in the butter until soft. Increase the heat, dust the steaks with flour, and brown them with the onions. Lift them out and keep warm.

3 Away from the heat, pour in the cognac and wine to prevent them igniting, then return to the stove and reduce to 1 tablespoon. Add the sliced bell pepper, tomato paste, cream, and broth. Boil together to form a sauce and return the meat to the pan. Serve the steaks with the sauce, garnished with the bell pepper.

Filet mignon steaks in phyllo pastry with *tapénade*

Tapénade is a Mediterranean appetizer, spread on toast or used as a dip. It can also be used to flavor the thin sheets of phyllo pastry, adding an extra dimension to this dish.

1 Make the *tapénade*: In a food processor blend the olives, tuna, anchovies, capers, and mustard to a smooth paste. Set aside.

2 Sear the tournados briefly on each side in a little butter and season. Let cool.

3 Lay out 4 sheets of the phyllo pastry and brush each generously with the melted butter, add a sprinkling of thyme, and a spread of the *tapénade*. Fold the pastry over to form a square and cut this into two halves down the middle. Wrap one of the steaks into each of these halves of pastry, and top with a spread of *tapénade*, to form a parcel. (You now have two parcels.) Repeat this process with the two remaining steaks. Cook for 15 minutes at 400°F until the pastry is crisp.

4 Serve with broiled vegetables (bell peppers, eggplant, zucchini) and Sauce béarnaise (page 36), or Mixed vegetable salad (page 54).

TAPÉNADE:

½ **cup olives, pitted**

4 oz canned tuna

3 anchovy fillets

1 Tbsp capers, drained and squeezed

2 tsp Dijon mustard

4 filet mignon steaks

8 sheets phyllo pastry

½ **stick butter, melted**

Dried thyme

Steak with onion gravy and Yorkshire pudding

Onion gravy is a delightful accompaniment to beef dishes.

ONION GRAVY:

3 medium onions, sliced thin

1 Tbsp vegetable oil

1 cup beef broth or gravy

2 tsp cornstarch mixed with
1 Tbsp water

Salt and pepper

4 Yorkshire puddings (page 60)

12 oz sirloin steaks, trimmed,
shredded, and seasoned

Oil, to fry

Fresh parsley, to garnish

1 Slowly cook the onions in the oil until soft, allowing them to color but adding a little water if they become too dark. This should take about a half hour. Add the broth or gravy and cornstarch mixture, bring to a boil, and simmer for 5 minutes. Season. There should now be 1¼ cups of onion sauce.

2 Preheat the oven to 450°F. To serve, reheat the Yorkshire puddings in the oven, then heat a griddle pan and add a little oil. When it is smoking toss in the seasoned steak and cook until just "roasted" on the outside. Remove the puddings from the oven, spoon a tablespoon of the onion sauce into each one, pile in the steak, and divide the rest of the sauce among the puddings. Serve with Horseradish sauce (page 36). Garnish with parsley.

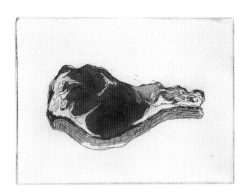

Fillet steaks with fresh tomato sauce on polenta cakes

Italians love colorful sauces and this is a good way to serve the awkward, uneven slices from the filet mignon end of the tenderloin. Do not be tempted to add extra flavorings to the polenta cakes recipe—there is enough flavor in the dish as it is.

At least 12 ¼-in thin fillet steaks

Salt and pepper

¼ cup olive oil

1 small red onion, chopped

2 garlic cloves, minced

3 Tbsp black olives, pitted and sliced

2 tsp chopped fresh marjoram

1 small can chopped tomatoes

Polenta cakes, to serve (page 60)

1 Season the steaks with salt and pepper. Place the oil and onion in a pan and heat gently until soft and light brown. Increase the heat and add the garlic, olives, marjoram, and tomatoes. Reduce to a thick, oily sauce.

2 Cook the steaks quickly on a very hot ridged griddle pan, turning once. Add them to the tomato sauce and baste them with it. Serve at once on top of hot Polenta cakes.

Stuffed filet mignon

The anchovy adds an interesting seasoning to the meat, helped by the cornichons and the garlic. Allow the steaks to marinate overnight and the flavor will be even better.

SAUCE:

½ stick butter

1 Tbsp olive oil

2 onions, chopped fine

2 garlic cloves, minced

⅔ cup white wine

4 medium tomatoes, peeled and seeded or 1 small can chopped tomatoes

1 bay leaf

¼ tsp dried marjoram

½ tsp dried thyme

Salt and pepper

4 filet mignon steaks weighing 7 oz each

2 garlic cloves

2 anchovy fillets cut into 1-in pieces

3 cornichons, sliced

5 black olives, pitted and sliced, to garnish

Green part of 2 scallions, sliced, to garnish

1 Heat the butter and oil together in a heavy pan, add the onion and garlic, and fry gently until soft. Add the wine and reduce until it has all disappeared into the onion mix. Stir in the tomatoes, bay leaf, marjoram, and thyme, season, and simmer for a further 5 minutes. Transfer the mixture to an ovenproof dish.

2 Preheat the oven to 400°F. Meanwhile, make several incisions all over the steaks with a sharp knife. Insert the garlic, anchovy, and cornichons randomly in them. Season the steaks and brown them carefully in the heavy pan then lay them over the tomato mixture. Cook in a hot oven for 8 minutes or until the steaks are done to your liking. Serve them with the sauce spooned around them. Garnish with the olives and scallions.

Fillet steak with root vegetables and dumplings

The traditional recipe for boiled beef and dumplings takes a long time to cook. Try this way and you can have the same effect in minutes. The glaze on the steaks turns this into a more sophisticated dish.

12 baby carrots

3 small turnips, quartered

12 small new potatoes

12 baby leeks

3 quarts beef broth

¼ stick butter

**4 fillet steaks, weighing
6 to 8 oz each**

¼ cup chopped fresh parsley

DUMPLINGS:

1¼ cups water

½ stick butter

2 heaping Tbsp flour

1 Tbsp semolina

1 tsp fresh thyme

2 small eggs

Seasoned flour, to roll

1 Cook the vegetables, refresh under cold running water, drain, and set aside. Season 5 cups of the broth and bring to a boil. Reduce the rest of the broth until it forms a glaze.

2 To make the dumplings bring the water to a boil with the butter. Stir in the flour, semolina, and thyme. Cook for 2 or 3 minutes until a ball is formed. Off the heat beat in the eggs one at a time. Season. Divide the mixture into 12 dumpling shapes and roll them in a little seasoned flour. Poach in boiling salted water for 10 minutes. Lift out with a slotted spoon and drain.

3 Bring the broth to a boil again and gently poach the steaks in it for 10 to 15 minutes adding in the dumplings for the last 5 minutes. Reheat the vegetables separately. Serve the steaks and dumplings with the vegetables spooned around. Pour the glaze over the meat and sprinkle with parsley.

Index